ENDORSEMENTS

Woodshop for Kids by Jack McKee is a breath of fresh air. The toys and activities available in today's world do not challenge children to be inventive or creative or to learn skills that are useful for meaningful work. Jack's book reflects a different view of children's capabilities and the kinds of activities that will engage their minds and enhance their confidence. **Woodshop for Kids** systematically and simply demonstrates how to help children of all ages use real tools and make useful objects. Any adult, whether knowledgeable about woodworking or not, will become a good teacher as well as a more skilled woodworker. Thanks, Jack, for putting us back on the right track in our work with children.
Deb Curtis, child care teacher, author, and adult educator.

Using only common building supplies and woodworking tools, kids will create and enjoy unique and easy-to-do wood projects requiring only basic woodworking skills and common sense safety rules. As the author of numerous creative art books, I am proud to highly recommend **Woodshop for Kids**, knowing that each child will benefit not only from pride in accomplishment and woodworking skills, but from tremendous fun and creativity!
MaryAnn F. Kohl, award-winning author and educational consultant, Bright Ring Publishing.

As a Montessori teacher, I am always looking for activities that encourage problem-solving, build independence and confidence, and allow for individual creativity. The projects in **Woodshop for Kids** are a perfect fit!
Kathie Wilson, Childlife Montessori School, Bellingham, WA.

Can I take this class?
A parent after helping in Jack's preschool shop class.

WOODSHOP for KIDS

52 Woodworking Projects Kids Can Build

684.08
M194w

JACK McKEE

Illustrations • Rusty Keeler

Woodshop for Kids:
52 Woodworking Projects Kids Can Build

Jack McKee
Copyright 2005 Jack McKee
First paperback edition 2005

Published by:
Hands On Books
1117 Lenora Court
Bellingham, WA 98225
phone: 360•671•9079
fax: 360•714•0774
email: mchkee@earthlink.net

Publishers Cataloging-in-Publication Data
McKee, Jack.
Woodshop for Kids: 52 Woodworking Projects Kids Can Build.
Author, Jack McKee; illustrations, Rusty Keeler;
book design, Paddy Bruce; editor, Jean Swanson;
photographs, Paddy Bruce and Jack McKee. — 1st ed.

1st ed.p. cm.
Includes bibliographical references and index.
LCCN 2005922022
ISBN-13: 978-1-884-894-53-4
ISBN-10: 1-884-894-53-4

1. Woodwork. 2. Woodworking tools. I. Keeler,
Rusty II. Bruce, Paddy. III. Swanson, Jean. IV. Title.

TT185.M34 2005   684'.08
QBI05-800232

Illustrations by Rusty Keeler
Book design by Paddy Bruce
Edited by Jean Swanson
Cover Photograph by Jennifer Fryer
Photographs by Paddy Bruce and Jack McKee

Acknowledgments

Many people, some without realizing it, helped me along the path to writing this book. Thank you.

Thanks to my sons, Ben and Andrew, who got me started working with kids. Thanks to all the kids I've helped with woodworking for their ideas, enthusiasm, humor, and for teaching me I could teach. Thanks to Molly Faulkner at Whatcom County Park's Roeder Home for giving me my first woodworking class. Thanks to Dana Hanks at the Roeder Home for supporting woodworking all these years. Thanks to Kathie and Steve Wilson at the Childlife Montessori school for trusting me with kids despite my lack of formal training.

Writing is one thing; turning it into an actual book is another and required lots of help. I'd like to thank family and friends who all seemed to show up at just the right time. Thanks to my wife, Candy Meacham, for putting up with me while I wrote this book and for advice along the way. Thanks to Jean Swanson (also my sister) for much needed editing. Thanks to Rusty Keeler for the wonderful illustrations. Thanks to longtime friend Paddy Bruce for the cover design, interior layout, and photographs. Thanks to MaryAnn Kohl for advice and encouragement when I needed it. Thanks to Jan Techter for typesetting and to Janey Bennett for proofreading. And thanks to Brett Lovins and Rob Maxwell for helping me deal with computer crises as they occurred.

TABLE OF CONTENTS

Preface

There is something magical about the process of building, the transformation of raw materials by knowledge, skill, and persistence into a useful and nice looking product. This book is about setting kids up to capture some of that magic.

If you don't have any woodworking experience, don't try to learn about all the tools at once. Find a project that interests your kids, see what tools are necessary, and then go back to the tool section and learn how to use them. It won't take long before you're an "expert" at building several projects and can transfer your new skills to kids.

For woodworkers, it's different. We have to think about all those little details we do without thinking. For me, this was the interesting part: what steps are actually involved in pounding a nail, cutting a board, using a drill, or laying out a project. Then, after you figure out what the steps are, you have to communicate them with one or two sentences so kids won't get lost in the verbiage.

Woodworking is great fun for kids but more important, they learn not be afraid of using tools and building. Kids from my preschool classes show up five years later and they have often forgotten the details of how to use tools but they still have the "I can build" attitude.

To my dad and grandfather for
teaching me to use tools.

INTRODUCTION
How I Started Working with Kids and Wood

It was a combination of being a stay-at-home Dad and the needs of a small fixer-upper house that got me started woodworking with kids. When I started, my construction experience consisted of building soapbox derby cars, forts, kites, and an arsenal of rubber band guns as a kid, plus reluctantly helping my Dad finish off the garage when I was a teenager. But I did have some friends who had worked on houses and cousins who'd built boats. Everyone said to jump right in and learn as you go. So I did. If I didn't know how to build a fence or a deck, I looked for one to copy or went to the library for plans. Our son Ben came along and my wife and I decided it made more sense for me to take care of him and work on our house than for me to get a job and pay for daycare and for someone to work on the house.

I had some help, too. My brother helped me frame an extra bedroom. Not only did I learn about framing, the permit process, wiring, roofing, and sheetrock, but I received a lesson in how much work it is to take care of a baby. After I added a room and a roof while taking care of Ben, I knew I could work through just about any building problem. Any kid problem, too.

Cousin Sid, Andrew and Ben looking out Andrew's future bedroom window.

Over the next couple of years I spent a lot of time taking care of Ben. I was always working on our house or building something and I learned he could be entertained by playing with tools like a clamp or hand drill. Not long after that, Ben started taking apart flashlights and faucets.

A little later, he wanted to "help" in my workshop. Ben saw me using a hot glue gun and wanted to try it himself. At first I was reluctant, but I let him try and he proved to me a $4^{1}/2$-year-old could be trusted to use hot glue. I got him started taking apart old radios and record players and he combined the leftover parts with hot glue. He began to make elaborate "space stations" for his action figures. Soon I realized I could trust him with a saw, which led to making pencil holders and key rings.

Later still, little brother Andrew came along and wanted in on the fun. He wanted to try my razor-sharp hand plane himself. His persistence finally overcame my reluctance. Much to my surprise, he was extremely careful and spent hours using every plane I possessed.

The kids were comfortable in the shop where I could watch them while getting some work done. As they grew older, woodworking became especially popular around birthdays and Christmas, when they found they could make valued gifts, have fun, and save money at the same time.

Andrew (right) and his friend Edward working on Pine Box cars at Edward's house. They should be wearing eye protection.

My First Woodworking Class

The excitement and interest of my own kids about using tools, about building, and about woodworking taught me how competent kids could be and inspired me to do volunteer woodworking at my sons' school. My plan was for the children to arrive with an idea of something to build and I would help them build it. From woodworking with my own kids, I knew enough to collect a workbench, kid-sized tools, and some scrap wood.

It turned out to be more complicated than I anticipated. Six kids arrived. Two had some idea about what to build and I was able to help them get started, even though I had to demonstrate a tool or help with a design problem. Some didn't know where to begin and I didn't know how to get them started. I tried to create, with words, an image of a project that would capture their interest. I asked, "Would you like to build a boat, (pencil holder, key ring)?" The answer came back something like, "maybe" or "let me think about it." Other kids had an idea about what to build but no clue how to begin, so I had to figure out construction details off the top of my head and communicate those details to the child in a way they could understand. No one got hurt. I didn't get mad or upset and make anyone hate woodworking, but the class was confusing for the kids and hectic for me. And not much was built. I went home to evaluate.

I had expected too much. Perhaps I made unconscious and unfair comparisons with my own children who had been around tools since birth. I had assumed kids could use a vice. They couldn't. I assumed they knew enough to keep their fingers away from the saw teeth. They didn't. Later I asked and none of the kids had ever used any tools before. How could they be expected to know what to do?

I needed to review the way I used tools to see if I could break down actions that I did automatically into steps kids could understand. I started with a safety demonstration: how to carry the saw, how to put a piece of wood in the vice, and how to use a saw. This was a step in the right direction and gave kids enough background to begin using tools without getting hurt. I became intrigued by the details of how to use tools at a beginning level. Over time, I refined this introductory demonstration and developed short lessons for each tool.

I was also expecting children who had never picked up a tool to be able to figure out what they wanted to make when the whole idea of making something was foreign. I decided to take a boat and a pencil holder my son had built to the second class to see if this would help the children visualize a project. When I showed the boat and pencil holder, the kids reacted with excitement and enthusiasm. Everyone wanted to build both a boat and a pencil holder. The class was still hectic, but it was amazing to me that a few tool lessons and a couple of projects could change the class tone from hectic and lost to interested and excited. Everyone went home with a project. The kids' enthusiasm was contagious and I went home and thought up more projects. I had so much fun, I began to wonder if there was some way to be paid for woodworking with kids.

I approached the local Park Department with the idea of a summer shop class for children. Even though I didn't have much teaching experience, they were enthusiastic. I, however, was more than a little unsure and nervous about how things would go. I wanted to duplicate the playful atmosphere that prevailed at home with my own boys. Would other kids respond? Could I keep them from hurting themselves? Would they be interested in the projects I had created?

That first year, half of the projects I developed were too complicated, but the other half worked surprisingly well and I was encouraged. We did a little bit of everything: woodworking, making folk toys, taking things apart, and doing experiments with electricity. The kids got a taste of the magic of building and experimenting and I got a taste of the magic of kids. Other children responded much like my own. They appreciated real tools and engaging projects. They worked hard to be safe. It was the most meaningful, fun, and interesting woodworking I'd ever done.

After that first summer class, I was asked to teach "shop" to 3-6 year olds at a Montessori school and ended up working there for six years. Since then, I've taught summer classes and helped older children build a variety of projects including cardboard domes, a take-apart playhouse, log buildings, and boats. It still amazes me how much youngsters love to build.

Why I Decided to Write a Book

Many adults seem interested in woodworking with kids but don't know where to start or what to expect. Parents of children in my classes asked how to set up woodworking at home for their children. I answered questions as best I could, but it is hard to explain many details in a few minutes' conversation. Preschool teachers were also interested. Once word got around that I did woodworking with kids, the local Washington Association for the Education of Young Children (WAEYC) asked if I would present a workshop for teachers.

School had not exactly been my forte and the thought of facing a room full of teachers was intimidating. Then I thought about a Montessori mom who had volunteered to help in "shop." After helping her daughter and others build pencil holders she asked, only half jokingly, "Can I take this class?" She had never had the opportunity to use tools and wanted to learn. Maybe teachers would feel the same way. I agreed to do the workshop and have been doing them ever since.

Even a 3-hour workshop is so short I have to leave things out. Sometimes I forget to mention details. Participants always ask for more written information, especially project ideas, to share with the rest of their staff. Several of my teacher students mentioned that if they only had a book with all the basic information, it would be easier to share information and obtain parental help.

So, in an effort to help anyone who has considered woodworking with children, I've compiled the answers to the questions I've been asked by parents and by workshop participants and put them in this book. I hope this information will make woodworking with kids easier and more pleasurable for others and, above all, I hope it will help more children have the opportunity to work with wood.

How to Use This Book

The first four chapters, Safety, Tools, Wood and Measuring, and Nails and Screws, are about what is involved in getting ready to do woodworking with kids. Read the Safety section carefully. Read about the tools necessary for the project you choose. The best way to start is one project at a time with just one or two kids. Quite a few projects can be started with just a few tools. After ten projects, tools and materials will accumulate and your shop will be ready for nearly any project.

Chapter Five, Projects, gives step-by-step details for 52 tried and true, kid-tested projects. Working out the details of project construction takes feedback from children. At first, about half the projects I offered were too complicated. With preschoolers especially, I had to keep telling myself, "simplify, simplify, simplify." Building a few of these projects will start kids down the path of designing projects of their own.

The Appendix contains a list of tools I've acquired for working with kids. Not all of these are required to begin. It also has a collection of tools you can build to make woodworking easier and activities that can be done in a living room or a classroom with very young children.

The Bibliography has a list of books pertinent to woodworking with kids. Plans for a playhouse and a boat kids can build with adult help are included after the Bibliography.

A Few Words About Hand Tools

This is a book about how to use hand tools with preschool and elementary age children. Hand tools are perfect for kids. They are safe if used properly, user-friendly, easy to find, and, when compared to power tools, inexpensive. They are quiet (sort of) and allow kids to exchange ideas as they work. Useful hand-tool skills can be acquired quickly and used throughout a lifetime. Nevertheless, people ask about using power tools with kids.

I can't imagine anyone would think of letting young children use high speed cutting tools like a table saw, circular saw, or router. Would you give them the keys to the car? But what about a battery drill or hand orbital sander? My advice is to help kids develop competence with hand tools before attempting any power tool.

For the projects in this book, there is no reason to use power tools. The purpose of using a power tool is to do repetitive jobs faster. If you have lots of holes to drill, screws to put in, or boards to sand, power tools are definitely handy. For a few holes or screws or boards, they aren't much help, not worth the added danger and hassle. It would be like letting a child ride a bike from one end of the house to the other just to get there faster.

Even battery drills can be quite powerful. It's quite easy to drill a hole in your hand (I've done it more than once) or twist a wrist or finger, or get hair caught in the chuck. They are serious tools. The orbital sander is noisy and produces a lot of airborne sawdust. For small jobs, hand sanding is easier.

When kids are in middle school you can consider the battery drill and orbital sanders. But in my opinion, there should be a good reason or a real advantage for using them. Here are two examples:

Several adults, including myself, helped 24 kids build six boats. We let kids use battery drills because there were hundreds of holes to drill. We dealt with the increased danger issue by having one adult supervising each boat (four kids). We didn't use the orbital sanders because there was plenty of labor; that is, there was no good reason for using it. If we had introduced sanders, there would have been one kid working and three standing around talking about who was to do the work. Even though there was quite a bit of sanding, with four kids hand sanding, the work was finished quickly and everyone was part of it.

I helped set up a project where 8th graders constructed a set of Builder Boards (see page 198) for the local women's care shelter. I had the kids use hand orbital sanders for sanding. There was an incredible amount of sanding and lots of other jobs too, so we had to think about efficiency. A dust collection system was in place, so we didn't have to worry about breathing sawdust.

Where to Get Help

If you are a woodworker, the tools, materials, and procedures in this book will be familiar.
I hope the information will keep you from having to reinvent the wheel, so to speak.

But if you have little or no woodworking experience, you will need some help to set up some projects. If you're a teacher, ask a parent or grandparent. In any group of 25 kids, I can almost guarantee someone will have a parent or relative interested in woodworking and willing to help.
A high school or middle school shop class could also assist. Other possibilities: the senior center, the volunteer center, or a place that sells recycled lumber.

Beginning

Anyone who is willing to spend some time setting up and then practicing using a few tools can help kids build nifty projects from wood. Don't think about "WOODWORKING." Think about the project in front of you. Build a few easy projects first. After a few projects, almost like magic, skills develop, patterns emerge, and you're thinking of alterations and projects of your own. It's the same process children go through, only adults learn faster. Many adults ask, "Is this all there is to it?" Building is learned by the experience of building. Woodworking is like cooking. Once you know how to make a peanut butter sandwich or pancakes, you can show someone else, and probably figure out how to make cookies on your own.

Woodworking is more than just woodworking. Because woodworking sometimes requires extra hands, kids learn to help each other and quickly become a small community. Ideas pass back and forth. Everyone realizes it isn't as easy to build as they thought and they gain an appreciation for the usefulness of tools. They begin to learn how to plan and organize a project and to solve problems when things don't go as expected. Children who at first want me to micromanage every step of a project become more self-reliant. Others in a hurry slow down and become more careful. Many kids who don't do well in school find they excel at building. Children realize people can actually make beautiful and useful things. And by the second or third day, kids actually listen when I explain construction details.

CHAPTER ONE · SAFETY

When my son Andrew was five years old, he loved hanging around the shop with me. He watched the curls come off the wood as I planed a board and wanted to try it himself. I showed him how the plane blade was adjusted, demonstrated how sharp the blade was by shaving hair off my arm, and explained how the plane straightened a crooked board edge. I was reluctant to let him handle the tool because of the sharp blade, but his enthusiasm and excitement convinced me to give him a chance. I told him to keep both hands on top of the plane and to put the plane down as soon as he was finished, figuring he couldn't cut himself if both hands were away from the blade. Over the next several days he spent hours using every plane in my shop, churning out curls, rounding corners, and straightening boards at a prodigious rate. From planes he moved on to saws. This experience taught me that even very young children can be trusted to use real tools. Fifteen years of woodworking with kids has confirmed this initial experience.

BEFORE KIDS ARRIVE: SETTING UP

Safe woodworking starts with proper setup. This includes a child-sized workbench, a vice, eye protection, appropriate tools, and a separate pounding area. After setup is complete and the children arrive, I give a quick tour of the shop and then explain how to carry tools and use the vice and saw. I'll show older kids how to use the drills, too. Once children know and understand safe procedures, the trick is to keep reminding them in a non-threatening manner until understanding is transformed into habit.

Workbench

Each child should have a proper-height workbench with enough space to work. One summer I saw a boat-building area for children at a maritime festival. Boat building with kids is a great idea, and the kids were having a good time, but the workbench was too high and there were too many children for the allotted space. I could hardly watch. One child had to reach so high to use a drill that her face was nearly the same level as the drill bit. Other children were using saws and hammers almost on top of each other. A lower table and more workspace would have made the event a great deal safer. Workbench dimensions and options are in the Appendix, page 182.

Woodworking Vice

At that same woodworking festival, I watched children cut dowels by holding the dowel in one hand and a saw in the other. I could see this was frustrating because the dowel moved with each stroke of the saw. It's also risky because little fingers were close to the moving saw blade. Putting the wood in a vice would have made cutting safer by allowing children to keep both hands on the saw handle, away from the saw teeth, and by keeping the wood steady. A vice also makes sawing easier and less frustrating. Details of the vice and how to use it start on page 16.

Saws

A small, sharp, fine-tooth saw is essential. See Saws, pages 20-23. Choose a saw 12-14" long with 12-14 teeth per inch. Avoid big saws, saws with less than 12 teeth per inch, and aggressive cutting "tool box saws." These saws will aggressively cut fingers as well as wood and make cuts harder to start. Smaller keyhole saws with a hacksaw blade are great for an introductory saw or for cutting dowels and other small wood.

Eye Protection

Children should wear eye protection. Safety glasses should have adjustable straps and lenses that are curved back to cover the side of the eye. The straps allow the safety glasses to be tightened so they will fit small heads properly and won't fall off. Extra-small safety glasses to fit children can be found at safety supply stores. Another source for eye protection is the large school supply catalogs. Many have the more traditional goggles. These work well, too. *Figure 1* shows several choices. I tell kids that goggles will take a little time to get used to but that soon they won't think about them.

Most children will wear goggles without complaint. I tell them my safety glasses have saved my eyes many times from globs of oil, wood splinters, metal shavings and sawdust. The rule is, "You must wear safety glasses in the shop." No exceptions. If exceptions are made, it is easy to become mired in endless judgment calls about whether a child should be wearing goggles. Out of ten kids,

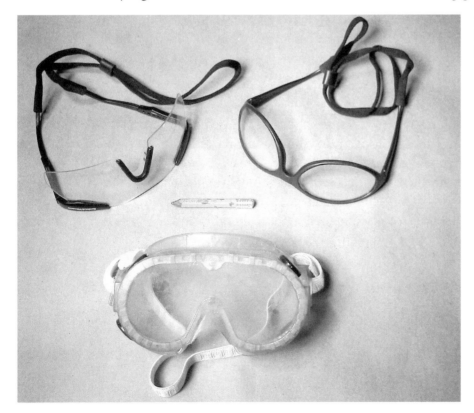

Figure 1.
Safety glasses or goggles provide eye protection.

maybe one or two will complain. If this happens, make sure the goggles aren't too tight or defective in some way. Have them try another pair or a different style. If they still complain, have a safe place they can "take a break" with their goggles off for a minute or two. Usually they will soon be back in shop with their goggles on.

Safe Pounding Area

Establish a separate hammering area removed from the workbench. Besides being aggravating to anyone nearby, hammering carries the possibility of flying pieces of wood or nails. A child wielding a hammer is usually not paying much attention to anything else. A large, flat, out-of-the-way stump makes a good solid surface for pounding. This separate pounding area will also protect other children from flying objects and the distraction of a neighbor pounding nails. One child at a time at the pounding block.

Hitting fingers with a hammer is another way children get hurt. Although it hurts, there is no lasting damage. Show children how to tap the nail to start it, then move their hand away, far away, before hitting the nail harder.

In spite of my best intentions, screws sometimes end up near the pounding block and children will try to pound them in with a hammer. This is not a good idea. Screws are designed to twist in and consequently require incredible amounts of force to drive with a hammer. They are also made from a harder steel so they tend to break rather than bend like a nail. This combination of harder steel and harder pounding can result in broken screws zinging around the room. Try to keep screws separate from nails and away from the pounding block. A mini lesson pointing out the difference between screws and nails will enlist a child's cooperation.

Electrical Protection: Ground Fault Interrupters (GFIs)

In my preoccupation with safety, I have visions of a child using the wire cutters we use for cutting popsicle sticks to cut, either by accident or curiosity, a glue gun cord. To prevent this remote possibility I tell everyone not to use the wire cutters, or scissors, or any other tool at the glue-gun station. Then I tether the wire cutters to a table so it can't possibly reach the glue guns. Lastly, to provide fail-safe protection, I plug the glue guns into ground fault interrupter (GFI) protected outlets. GFIs are special electrical plugs commonly found in bathrooms, which turn the electricity off in case of a short or malfunction. They are inexpensive and easy to have installed.

AFTER KIDS ARRIVE

How to Carry Tools

The first danger comes from carrying tools. It is easy for a child to poke herself or someone else. In fifteen years of woodworking with children this has never happened in my class, but it could have. Unless children have been shown otherwise, a child carrying a tool will often aim the point straight ahead or toward his own face. Points of saws, drills, screwdrivers, chisels, or any other tool should be aimed down, away from your face and body, away from your friend's face and body, toward the floor. Saws should be carried parallel to the leg. Children should not run while carrying tools, or in a shop at all, for that matter. Demonstrate the correct way to hold tools and then be vigilant. Repeat safety advice. "Use it (the tool) or put it down," is a good rule.

Saw/Vice Demonstration

Figure 2 shows what not to do. Experienced woodworkers often use a saw by placing the wood on a low bench and holding it with their knee or one hand. The thumb of the hand holding the wood guides the saw and the other hand moves the saw back and forth. Young children want to do the same thing. While it's a good method for an experienced person, it is dangerous for a young beginner because it's difficult to hold the wood still, guide the saw, and start the saw cut all at the same time. Because beginners push down too hard, the saw can jump out of the cut and land on a thumb or finger. This can happen even to an experienced carpenter.

Beginners should put the wood in a vice (so it won't move) and keep both hands on the saw handle, away from sharp saw teeth. Later, after children have gained experience sawing wood in a vice, they can try the other way but they should clamp the wood to hold it still and wear a leather glove to protect the hand guiding the saw.

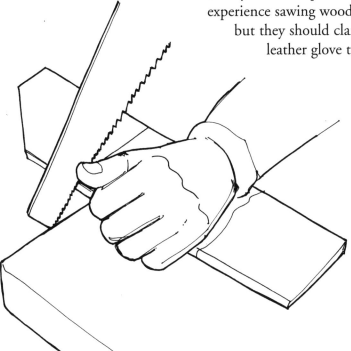

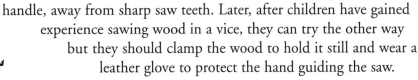

Figure 2.
This illustration shows what children should NOT do. An experienced woodworker holds the wood with one hand and guides the saw with his thumb. For beginners, especially kids, this risks the saw jumping out of the cut onto the thumb. I have kids use a vice to hold the wood and keep both hands on the saw handle. Later, after kids have gained experience sawing wood in a vice they can try the other way, using a leather glove to protect their thumb.

Rules

Woodworking requires children to remember many new things. It is unrealistic to expect they will remember everything related to safety the first time. Reminders are necessary. I couch these reminders in terms of safety, not in terms of breaking a rule: "I'm afraid if you run in the shop you'll get hurt." "If you're goofing around, the saw might accidentally cut your friend." "If we don't sweep up this sawdust, someone might slip." Children see these rules make sense. A big part of being a woodworking teacher is internalizing these rules (posting them on the wall won't help) and dishing them out at appropriate times. If you've set things up right and done careful demonstrations, kids will respond. Here are my rules:

- Two hands on saw handle
- Use it or put it down
- No open toe shoes; in other words, no sandals or flip flops
- Clean up after each work period or more frequently if necessary
- No fooling around
- No running
- Wear goggles
- Long hair should be tied up (good habit for future power tool users)
- Put the wood in a vice before sawing or drilling

Figure 3.
Billy (standing) and Parker help during clean up time.

Airborne Sawdust

Today, with childhood asthma on the increase, and with the knowledge that severe allergic reactions to airborne sawdust have occurred in adults, I'd feel remiss if I didn't mention allergic reaction to wood. I don't know of any scientific research pertaining specifically to children and exposure to sawdust. I assume information about adults is also valid with children, probably to a greater extent. Before I scare everyone, it seems that given the small amount of sawdust children produce and the short time they are exposed to it, the risk is no more, and probably much less, than for other airborne particles children might be exposed to. Nevertheless, for a child with a chemical sensitivity or with asthma, reactions to wood dust are conceivable. The following information is also important for the person preparing materials, whose exposure is considerably more than for children.

When wood is sawn or sanded, especially with power tools, minute particles of wood dust go into the air and can be inhaled. Long-term exposure to these particles can cause respiratory problems. To keep from breathing wood dust, professional woodworkers are required to have dust collection systems which suck sawdust from stationary tools and filter the air. These systems help tremendously, but it's impossible to collect all the airborne sawdust, especially from tools like the circular saw, router, and hand sander, which put far more sawdust in the air than a child sanding. To protect against this localized sawdust, woodworkers wear, or should wear, a properly fitting dust mask. On construction sites where there is no dust collection system, dust masks (respirators are better) are important, especially when cutting chemically treated woods which contain poisons, and plywood or particle board which contain toxic glues. It is only prudent to take as many precautions as possible. If you don't have a dust collection system, work outside and wear a dust mask. Certainly for children, treated wood should be avoided and cutting plywood should be kept to a minimum because of toxic glues.

When children start using power sanders and other power tools (as they do in some middle school shop classes) a dust collection system should be in place and students should wear a dust mask.

In the short term, wood dust particles can cause mild reactions or hypersensitive reactions. Mild reactions (also called irritant reactions) are like hives, itching, or welts. Although I've never encountered a child with a mild reaction, I have a friend for whom fir is an irritant. Soon after coming into a room where fir has been sawn or sanded, her eyes and arms begin to itch. If she sticks around, welts appear on her arms. Her reaction subsides soon after she leaves the area where fir is being worked with. Many other woods cause similar reactions, so be on the lookout for hives, welts and extreme itching.

Just as a very few people are hypersensitive to chemicals, peanuts, or bee stings, a person can be hypersensitive to a particular wood. These reactions are extremely rare. If it is known a child is hypersensitive to wood dust of any kind, I would be very hesitant to have them in woodworking class.

As a teacher (or parent), prepare as you would for a child hypersensitive to bee stings by being aware of the possibilities, keeping the phone and emergency telephone numbers handy, and taking first aid training. Avoid using tropical hardwoods like cocobolo, ebony, and iroko, which cause more reactions than domestic woods.

A young child with asthma might be more sensitive to wood dust than someone who doesn't have asthma. Consult parents. Perhaps an extra small dust mask could be used. Another option is a sanding box. This is a shallow box, with a wire screen top, hooked to a shop-vac. If sanding is done over the box most of the sawdust goes into the box and then to the shop-vac instead of going into the surrounding air. Put the shop-vac outside to reduce noise.

Woodworking does have the potential to be dangerous. Knowledgeable supervision, appropriate tools, and good habits make it safe. Children quickly see the connection between unsafe use of tools and injury. They work hard to follow rules. Children love woodworking and it is amazing to watch how safety-conscious, interested, and motivated a child can be. Use the proper setup, show them how to safely use tools, remind them when they forget, help them when they need it, and watch the creations materialize.

CHAPTER TWO · TOOLS

THE WORKBENCH

Nothing makes woodworking more difficult and irritating than a work area that is too high, too low, or moves with every stroke of the saw. Child-sized workbenches can be found in school supply catalogs, but they are expensive. The large home improvement centers often have workbenches which are less expensive but serviceable if the legs are cut down so the top is a more appropriate height for children. Another option is a homemade workbench which makes a good project for an interested parent. See the Appendix, page 182 for plans.

A workbench should not move. The first time I did woodworking with preschoolers, I had a nice solid oak bench but it wasn't fastened down. An enthusiastic preschooler with a saw could unintentionally move the bench enough to block access to the project shelf or the wood box. After I fastened it to the concrete floor, it was easier for a child to saw and less disrupting for everyone else. Another time, fastening to the floor was not an option, so I added a sturdy plywood shelf under the workbench top and stacked about 100 pounds of concrete blocks on it. This did the job, too.

A woman who took my woodworking workshop sent me an e-mail asking if I had plans for a woodworking workbench. I sent her the plans in the Appendix. When she sent a picture of her bench, it was nothing like the plans. It was better. She had used 4 X 4s for the legs and varnished the whole bench. It was beautiful *(Figure 4)*. The workbench plans in the Appendix are for the easiest sturdy bench I could design. If you want something fancier, go to the library or the internet and search for "workbench plans."

Figure 4.
Kathy Baker's workbench.

THE VICE

Like most novices, children have difficulty beginning to use a saw because they must keep track of many things at the same time: holding the wood, moving the saw, starting the cut, keeping the saw straight. A vice to hold the wood allows the young woodworker to focus on manipulating the saw. It enables both of the child's hands to be placed on the saw handle—away from the saw teeth—making sawing safer. For similar reasons, a vice makes drilling holes, sanding, and using a plane all easier and safer.

Although there are exceptions, whether children are sawing, sanding, or drilling, I tell them, "hold the wood still." If you hold a piece of wood in one hand and sand it with the other, most of your energy goes into moving the wood, not sanding it. Put the wood in a vice and that wasted energy goes directly to sanding. Using a plane requires a vice to hold the wood so that both hands can be kept on the top of the plane, away from the sharp plane blade.

Woodworking Vice Versus the Metalworking Vice

There are two basic types of vices. One is designed for woodworking; it has large wooden jaws (which don't come with the vice) to hold soft pieces of wood tight without marring them. The other type is designed for working with metal. It has small hardened steel jaws with rough surfaces for grasping nuts, bolts, and pieces of metal. These hardened jaws will crush, or leave marks on, any softwood clamped between them. *Figure 5a* shows the woodworking vice; *Figure 5b* shows the metalworking vice.

While this may seem obvious, a woodworking vice is the best choice. It does a better job of holding the odd-size and -shaped pieces of wood children will be using. I only mention the metalworking vice because I have seen many used with kids and some school supply catalogs even sell them for use in children's woodworking classes. Whatever type of vice you have, making plywood inserts to fit over the steel jaws, as explained below, will make it more serviceable. Without wood inserts, not only will the metal jaws mar the wood, but more importantly, children will cut into the metal of the vice and quickly dull the saw. Here is how to make extra large inserts:

Figure 5a. *Woodworking vice.*

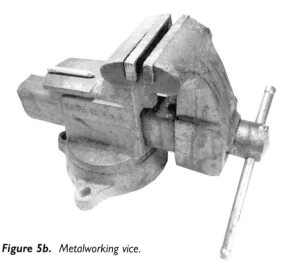

Figure 5b. *Metalworking vice.*

Making Inserts for the Woodworking Vice

Tools

- Surform plane.
- Countersink.
- Hand or battery-powered drill, 3/16" drill bit, 1/2" drill bit.
- Screwdriver and small adjustable wrench to fit bolts holding inserts to vice.

- Handsaw.

Materials

- Four 1 1/2" flathead bolts 3/16" in diameter with nuts and lock washers.
- A 12" X 12" piece of 1/2" plywood will be enough plywood unless you have a giant vice.
- Sandpaper, about 80 grit.

Usually inserts are even with the vice jaws, but in children's shop, it is important to have them stick out beyond the metal of the vice on both the top and sides. This way, if a child's attention wanders, the saw will cut into the replaceable wood inserts instead of the metal of the vice. *Figures 6a and 6b* show how the inserts fit into the vice.

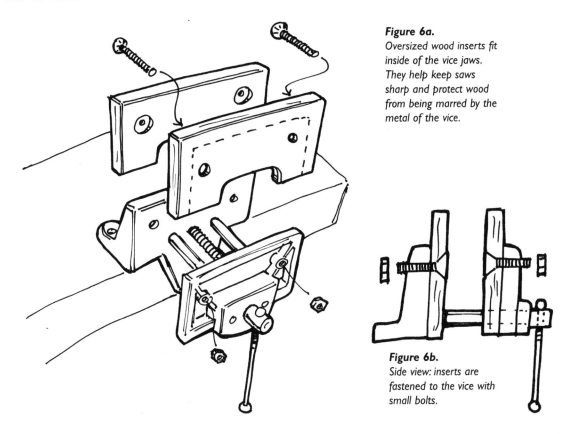

Figure 6a.
Oversized wood inserts fit inside of the vice jaws. They help keep saws sharp and protect wood from being marred by the metal of the vice.

Figure 6b.
Side view: inserts are fastened to the vice with small bolts.

Construction

1. Cut two pieces of $^{1}/2$" plywood $1^{1}/4$" wider and $^{5}/8$" taller than the vice jaws. Make a cutout or drill holes for the vice guide(s) and threads as shown in *Figure 6a*.

2. Put both inserts into the vice and clamp the vice shut. Make sure the top and sides of the inserts are even and that at least $^{5}/8$" of wood protrudes beyond the vice. Holes are provided in the vice for attaching inserts. Use these holes as guides for drilling holes in the inserts.

3. After drilling the holes, open the vice and fasten the inserts to the inside of the respective vice jaw with small ($^{3}/16$") flathead bolts. Make sure the bolt heads on the inside of the vice sink below the surface of the wood or each piece of wood inserted into the vice will come out with an imprint of the screw head. Sometimes you can just tighten the nuts down enough so the screw heads are pulled below the surface of the wood. Other times the hole for the bolt heads must be enlarged with a countersink (see countersinking, pages 46-47) or large drill bit.

4. After the inserts are fastened to the vice, close the vice tightly and check to make sure the tops and sides of the inserts are still even. Plane them down with the Surform plane, if necessary, until they match.

Making Inserts for the Metalworking Vice

Figure 7 shows a metalworking vice with plywood inserts. Two pieces of plywood are cut to fit over the top of the existing steel vice jaws and held in place with longer screws through the same holes that keep the steel jaws in place.

Figure 7.
Wood inserts are mounted on top of the standard metal jaws of a metalworking vice. Wood insert pattern is in the foreground.

Tools

- Handsaw.
- Vice.
- Sandpaper.
- Drill and bit to match the size of screws holding the jaws to the vice.
- Keyhole or coping saw for making the bottom cut on the insert.
- Screwdriver to match screws holding jaws to vice.
- Surform plane.
- Countersink.

Materials

- Two 6" X 6" squares (more or less depending on size of vice) of $1/2$" plywood.
- Four screws, with the same threads, and about $1/2$" longer than the screws holding the vice jaws.

Construction

1. From $1/2$" plywood, cut replacement jaws that stick out at least $3/4$" beyond the metal of the vice. The wood in front of the vice in *Figure 7* shows the shape of the inserts for my vice. Your vice may be different.
2. After the inserts are cut out, put them in the vice and close the vice. Draw around the jaws, onto the inserts. This marks where the inserts will fit the jaws. Open the vice and remove the inserts.
3. Remove screws holding the vice jaws in place. Use the new longer screws with the same thread pattern.
4. Put each jaw on top of its matching insert in the outline made in step #2. Use the holes in the jaws to mark the position for the holes in the inserts. Drill holes in the inserts.
5. Fasten the wood inserts to the vice over the top of the jaws. Countersink the screw heads so they will be below the surface of the wood on the inside of the vice.
6. Make the tops of the two inserts even by planing with a Surform.

Using a Vice

At first it is hard for children to remember which direction to turn the vice handle. As a reminder paint two arrows, one clockwise and one counterclockwise, along with the appropriate word, "open" or "close", near the vice handle. Activities like the little hammer, the screwdriver work, or the faucet (see Mechanical Puzzles, pages 192-196) will help hands remember before kids understand word cues like "righty tighty," "lefty loosey" or "clockwise" which are sometimes helpful for older children. I tell students to watch the vice jaws as they turn the handle: one direction opens, the other closes. This enables a child to figure out for herself whether she is turning the correct direction or not.

Occasionally kids turn the vice handle counterclockwise until the threads are disengaged. When this happens the vice won't open or close and the front half of the vice may fall to the floor. This can be quite a surprise. Once a child in my class felt bad because he mistakenly thought he had broken the vice. The unattached vice jaw can be rethreaded by an older child or the teacher. Point to the arrow and gently remind them to watch which direction the jaws move as they turn the handle.

The next step is to give the child a piece of wood to put in the vice "as tight as you can get it." Have her try to move the wood; if it moves, the vice needs to be tighter. Three- or four-year-olds may need a "cheater bar," a piece of pipe that slips over, and extends, the vice handle, providing more leverage. A 12" section of 1" water pipe will work. In addition, the vice handle (which slides back and forth) should not end up underneath the saw where it can collide with and dull the saw teeth. Once the wood is secure in the vice and the vice handle is not in the way, the student is ready for the saw lesson.

SAWS

Choosing a good handsaw and knowing how to use and care for it are critical for successful woodworking. Choosing the right saw can be confusing, too, because a good hardware store can have 25 different kinds of handsaws, many of which are not appropriate for kids. The following information will help sort out the basics.

Choosing a Saw

An appropriate saw for kids may be found at a good hardware store but eventually it will become dull and have to be taken to a saw shop (look under "saws" in the yellow pages) to be re-sharpened. If you are unfamiliar with saws, I recommend skipping the hardware store and going directly to a saw shop to purchase a saw. In addition to selling saws, they have the equipment to sharpen, set, and recut the teeth of handsaws. Sometimes they will have used saws for sale and, as I'll explain later, an older used saw may be better than a new one. They can show you how to tell a sharp saw from a dull one.

A good saw for kids is a crosscut saw, 14-22" long, that has 12 to 14 teeth per inch *(Figure 8)*. A crosscut saw cuts across a board, which is what most cutting is. It has different shaped teeth from a rip saw which cuts the length of a board. Different saws have different numbers of teeth per inch. I tell children, "big teeth for big wood; small teeth for small wood." For example, to cut a ¹/₄" dowel, an 18 tooth per inch saw (a hacksaw) would be a good choice, but to cut a 2 X 4, a saw with 8 teeth per inch would be about right. If you switched saws and attempted cutting the 2 X 4 with the 18 tooth saw, it would work but would take a long time. The 8 tooth saw would rip the ¹/₄" dowel to

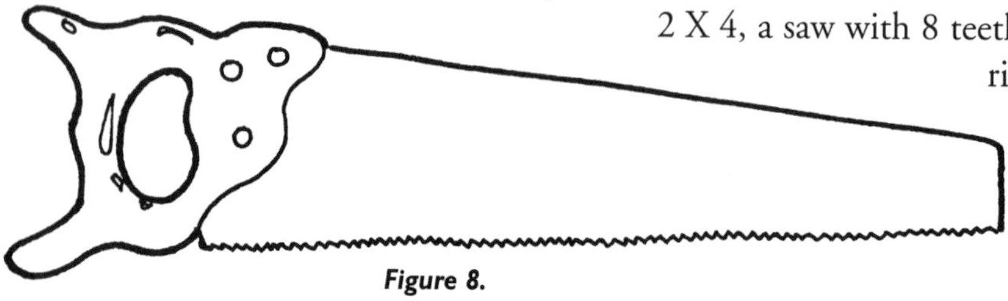

Figure 8.
A good saw for young children is about 14" long and has 12 to 14 teeth per inch.

shreds. While it might be a little coarse for the dowel and a little fine for the 2 X 4, a 12 to 14 tooth saw is a good compromise and will work for both.

Avoid saws with less than 12 teeth per inch; they are too coarse for the smaller pieces of wood children will be using. Stay away from the small "aggressive cutting" tool box saws that cut on both the pull and the push of a stroke; they aggressively cut fingers as well as wood and their large teeth make starting a cut more difficult. If you already have an "aggressive cutting" saw, a saw shop can grind the large teeth off and replace them with smaller teeth more appropriate for children. Another factor to consider is whether or not the saw blade has a taper.

A tapered saw *(Figure 9)* is thicker on the bottom of the blade by the teeth than at the top of the blade. It also tapers from handle to tip, being thinner at the tip and thicker at the handle. A saw with a tapered blade does not bind in the cut as much as a saw with a blade of uniform thickness. A tapered saw is less frustrating for children (or anyone) so it is nice to have at least one tapered saw for a child's first cuts, as well as for longer, more difficult cuts. Unfortunately, tapered saws are getting harder to find. A saw shop will probably know where to order one. I was able to find several tapered saws on the internet, but they were expensive.

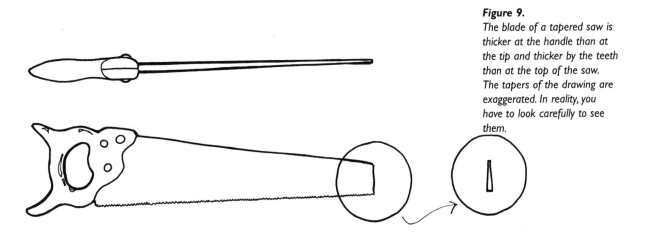

Figure 9.
The blade of a tapered saw is thicker at the handle than at the tip and thicker by the teeth than at the top of the saw. The tapers of the drawing are exaggerated. In reality, you have to look carefully to see them.

Used tapered saws can sometimes be found at saw shops or at garage sales. Look for a saw with a nice handle. The handle quality often reflects the quality of the blade. To recognize a tapered blade, look from the tip of the blade back toward the handle. The metal will be slightly thicker by the teeth than at the top of the blade. A non-tapered blade will be of uniform thickness. The top of the blade (opposite the teeth) will also taper, being thicker by the handle than at the tip. While these differences seem slight, they do make a difference, giving beginners a needed boost.

It doesn't matter if a garage sale saw is dull, as it most likely will be, or if the teeth are too coarse. They can be re-cut and sharpened at the saw shop. Some surface rust is OK, but avoid rust pits as they will cause the saw to bind. I have found many good saws at bargain prices.

Keeping a Saw Sharp

Once my son Ben was cutting rigging wire for his sailboat with a hacksaw. It cut well at first but later he complained it was taking a long time to get through one wire. When I looked, I could see the teeth on the hacksaw had been worn down to bumps. A determined person can cut with just about any saw, but a sharp saw will save a lot of frustration, not to mention work. I have made similar mistakes myself. Now I automatically check to see if a saw is sharp before I use it.

Eventually you learn to sense if a saw is sharp by the way it moves through the wood. A sharp saw glides. It almost seems to cut by itself. A dull saw seems to take forever to finish a cut. A dull saw makes a person grumpy.

Another way to tell if a saw is sharp is by looking (a magnifying glass helps) at the tip of each saw tooth as shown in *Figure 10*. **Be careful!** The teeth of a freshly sharpened saw should be razor sharp. **Don't test sharpness with your fingers!** Turn the saw over and carefully examine the points of each tooth. The teeth of a dull saw appear like a row of tiny bright spots because the points of the teeth are slightly rounded (dull) and therefore reflect light. If the saw is sharp, each tooth will come to a sharp point which won't reflect light so no bright spots appear.

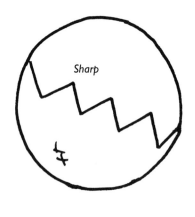

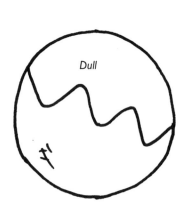

Figure 10.
The teeth of a sharp saw come to a sharp point which won't reflect light. The teeth of a dull saw are rounded (a larger surface area than a sharp point) and will reflect light. Dull saw teeth look like a row of tiny bright spots at the point of each saw tooth.

Once a saw is sharp, care must be taken to keep it sharp. Saw teeth should not come into contact with anything metal. For example, a saw should not be put down on a metal stool or put into a tool box without some sort of blade protection. Saws should not be stacked on top of one another or on other tools. They can be stored hanging on a peg, upright in a box with spacers between the blades, or inside a sleeve made from cardboard and duct tape.

You need to be vigilant to help kids keep their saws from touching metal and becoming duller. Be sure the vice handle slides to the side opposite the saw. Put away tools that aren't being used. Watch carefully to make sure children don't cut right through the inserts into the vice.

Introductory Saw Lesson

There are quite a few steps involved in using a saw. My approach is to provide the basics in an introductory lesson. This lesson includes safety information and gets kids using the saw:

1. Explain how to hold and carry the saw parallel to the leg (page 11, "How to Carry Tools").
2. Show how not to cut and explain why (page 11, "Saw/Vice Demonstration").
3. Demonstrate how to use the vice to hold the wood (page 19, "Using a Vice").
4. Have the child put a piece of wood in the vice as tight as he can clamp it. If it moves, it's too loose. Even though wood starts out tight, it may work loose. Instead of stopping and readjusting the wood, and retightening the vice, kids frequently try to finish the cut with the wood sloping at an odd angle. It is easier and more efficient to straighten the wood out and retighten the vice. The first time or two I'll do it for them. It only takes a few seconds, and they immediately feel how much easier it is to cut vertically. Words don't help much, and it is easy to lose a child's attention with an explanation. After a demonstration, he will do it correctly himself because experience has shown it is easier.
5. To start a cut, keep both hands on the saw handle. While saws do most of their cutting on the forward stroke, a cut is started on the back stroke. Pull the saw back a few times (lifting it on the forward stroke) to start the cut, then push gently back and forth, without pushing down, until the cut is well established.
6. Put the saw on the table as soon as the cut is finished. This is an important safety consideration. "Use it or put it down."

Helpful Hints

As children gain competence, add suggestions from the hints below:

1. After the cut is started, push down, just a little, on the forward stroke; relax on the back stroke. Every beginner pushes down too hard. Concentrate on moving the saw back and forth and keeping the saw straight, not pushing down.
2. Sight along the top of the saw to keep it straight. If the saw bends to one side, it binds and is harder to push. Candle wax rubbed on each side of the saw blade will help it glide through the cut. **Be careful. Keep fingers away from the saw teeth when applying the wax!**
3. At the end of a cut, don't push down at all. Just move the saw gently back and forth. Pushing down at the end of a cut will split the last part of the cut, *(Figure 11a)* leaving a large splinter, rather than a clean cut *(Figure 11b)*. When a cut does not split out at the end, a child is applying the right amount of downward pressure.
4. The saw teeth should be on the line. Watch the teeth of the saw where they meet the line

you are trying to cut. If the saw begins to deviate from the line, cut more with the tip of the saw and twist the handle (as it moves back and forth) slightly back towards the line. The trick is not to let the saw teeth get too far from the line before correcting.

Figure 11a.
Splinters at the end of a cut are caused by pushing down too hard on the saw.

Figure 11b.
A clean cut, without large splinters, comes from pushing down just the right amount.

Sawing is learned from practice. I tell the kids finesse is more important than power. While these pointers help, there are a lot of things to remember and do, all at the same time. When kids are first learning to saw, above all I stress safety. Next I make sure they have the wood tight in the vice and two hands on the saw. I try to get them to keep the saw straight, and I don't worry about the rest. When they're tired, I'll remind them to conserve energy by not pushing down so hard. After they've made a few projects, some children will begin to notice their cuts aren't straight. This is the perfect time to show them how to twist the handle of the saw to bring the cut back to the line.

Sawing Problems & Tricks

Cutting Too Far from the Vice

Saw cuts should be made with the cut right up close, almost against, the vice inserts. The farther a cut is from the vice, the more the wood will vibrate. The more it vibrates, the harder it is to cut. The smaller the wood the bigger the problem. A 1/4" dowel, for example, will be nearly impossible to cut 4" out away from the vice. It is dangerous, too, if the child takes one hand off the saw and attempts to keep the wood from moving. The solution is easy to demonstrate. I'll say, "Can I show you something?" I'll quickly loosen the vice and move the saw cut right up next to the vice. The child feels immediately how much easier the sawing becomes.

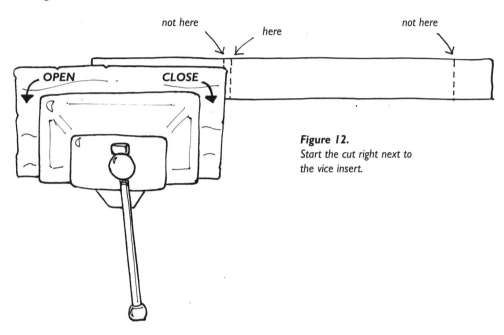

not here   *here*   *not here*

OPEN   CLOSE

Figure 12.
Start the cut right next to the vice insert.

Cutting Thin Pieces of Wood

This is really the same problem as above but in a slightly different form. As the wood becomes larger, it is sometimes logistically impossible to fit it into the vice with the cut near the inserts. With stiff thicker pieces of wood, like a 2 X 4, it doesn't matter, but thin pieces of wood, plywood for example, will vibrate back and forth so much they are hard to cut.

One way to address this problem is to sandwich the thin wood between two back-up strips before it's put in the vice. Place back-up stiffener strips even (and parallel) with the edge of the inserts and 1/8" back from the cut as shown in *Figure 13*. A small clamp may be necessary to hold the two backing strips together at the top. Keep the clamp and clamp handle out of the

Figure 13.
One way to cut a thin piece of wood is to sandwich it between two thicker pieces of wood. The clamp at the top makes sure the wood is held tightly at the top. Be careful not to cut into the clamp.

saw path. This operation is a little tricky
for younger kids to set up, so you will
probably have to do it.

Another method is to clamp the
wood between the top of a small wood
stool or workbench and a stiffener
(Figure 14). The clamp and the stiffener
provide halfway points to the traditional
way of holding the wood with your
hand or knee. Keep the clamp handle
out of the way of the saw teeth by
turning the clamp upside down so the
handle is underneath the work being
clamped.

After practice, older kids may no
longer need the clamp and stiffener and
can try this: First have the child wear a
small leather glove to protect his hand.

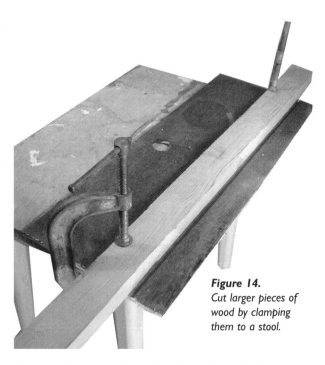

Figure 14.
*Cut larger pieces of
wood by clamping
them to a stool.*

The glove should be on the left hand for right-handers and the right hand for left-handers.
This gloved hand will guide the saw to begin the cut. The thumb should be held as high on
the saw blade as he can reach and the fingers should be tucked under the hand, like a fist
with the thumb sticking out and up as shown in *Figure 15.*

Figure 15.
*After wood is clamped
to a stool, have the
child put on a small
leather glove to protect
his thumb as it guides
the saw.*

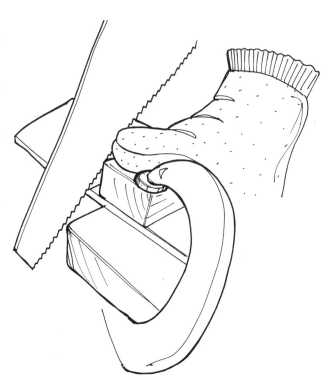

Angle Cuts

Because it is considerably easier to use a saw when the blade is vertical than when it is at an angle, wood should be placed in the vice with the cut straight up and down. For example, the easiest way to cut the bow of a boat is to put the wood in the vice at 45 degrees and cut the first side of the bow point. The cut should run straight up and down parallel to, and almost against, the vice insert. If the cut starts just below the top of the insert there will be a small notch between the wood and the vice insert, perfect for starting the saw cut *(Figure 16)*. For the second cut, move the wood to the other side of the vice (again at 45 degrees) and repeat the whole operation.

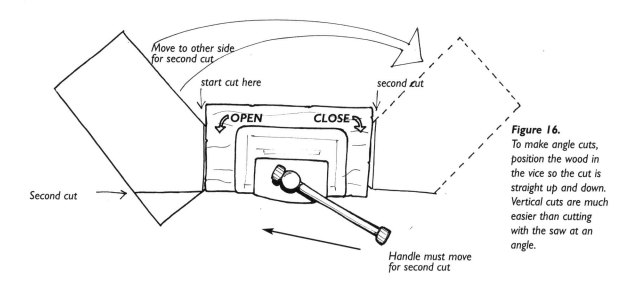

Figure 16.
To make angle cuts, position the wood in the vice so the cut is straight up and down. Vertical cuts are much easier than cutting with the saw at an angle.

Reminders

To help kids remember, I've made up some reminders:

- Two hands on the saw
- Turn the wood, not the saw
- Saw close to the vice
- Finesse, not power
- Watch the vice jaws (to see which way they are moving)

- Hold the wood still
- Don't push down so hard
- Use it or put it down
- Big wood big teeth, little wood little teeth

The Keyhole Saw

A keyhole saw *(Figure 17)* is designed to cut in small spaces, but I have kids use it for cutting small pieces of wood. It has replaceable blades. Either wood cutting blades (big teeth) or hacksaw blades (small teeth) are available. I don't use the wood cutting blades. The hacksaw blades are designed to cut metal, but are perfect for cutting small pieces of wood. The keyhole saw (with a hacksaw blade) is a good tool for a very young child's first lesson. When a child uses the larger 12-point crosscut saw to cut a small piece of wood like a dowel, he often breaks, or splits off, the last part of the cut because he is pushing down too hard. The keyhole saw with a hacksaw blade will result in a smoother cut.

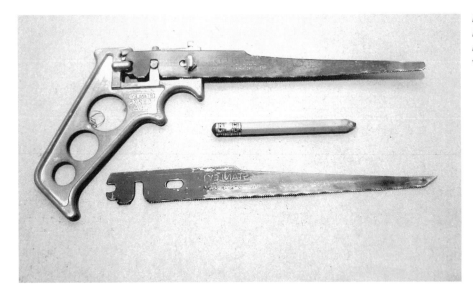

Figure 17.
I use hacksaw blades, not the bigger tooth wood cutting blades.

If you use a keyhole saw with a hacksaw blade as it is meant to be used, for cutting metal (thumb piano project), here is a trick that will make the blade last longer: don't press down as you pull the saw back. In fact, it's a good idea to lift the saw a bit on the back stoke. Pushing down on the back stroke knocks the sharp points off the tip of each saw tooth. A hacksaw blade will last many times longer if you lift it on the backstroke.

The Back Saw

The back saw has teeth like a crosscut saw but it has a metal stiffener along the top to prevent it from bending from side to side. It is used mostly in a miter box or block and should have 12-14 teeth per inch. Although the crosscut saw will work in a miter box, the back saw cuts straighter because it will not bend. If a child is having difficulty holding a saw straight, have her try a back saw.

The Rip Saw

The rip saw is convenient at times but not absolutely necessary. It will cut along the grain much faster than a crosscut saw. The teeth are extra coarse and have a special design. If a child can saw with a crosscut saw he can usually handle a rip saw. I keep it on a high shelf so I can review safety before use. When the student is finished cutting, it goes back on the shelf out of reach.

The Coping Saw

A coping saw is used for cutting curves. The body of a coping saw is a U-shaped metal frame. The open end of the U is spanned by a thin blade which will follow a curve without binding. It is a difficult saw for children to use because, in addition to the back and forth motion of a typical saw, a coping saw adds the challenge of turning as you cut. Second or third graders can acquire the skill if they are motivated, and the occasional kindergartner will catch on.

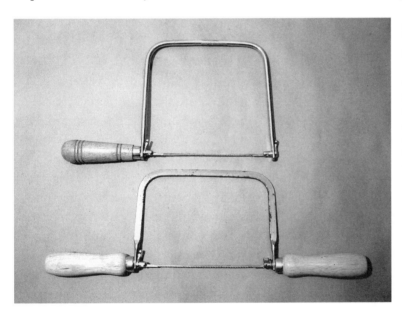

Figure 18.
The top saw is a standard coping saw. The bottom saw, assembled from two coping saws, is Jack's special two-handled coping saw for kids. It allows an adult to help without completely taking over.

To make it easier to learn, I put together a coping saw with two handles *(Figure 18)*, one for me and one for the student. This enables a child to follow my lead until he gets the feel of it. It also allows me to come back and straighten out a cut or help a bit without completely taking over. To make one of these helpful two-handled saws, combine two coping saws by removing the handle from one and installing it in place of the blade holder on the second saw.

Broken or dull coping saw blades can be replaced. A medium blade, about 18 teeth per inch, is about right unless trying to cut very thin wood. Then you'll need more teeth. A blade can be installed with the teeth pointing towards the handle or away from the handle. If the teeth point away from the handle, the saw will cut on the push stroke and if they point towards the handle, the saw will cut as it's pulled back. Either way works. Periodically rubbing a little candle wax on the blade will make the blade slide through the cut easier.

How to Change Coping Saw Blades

Coping saw blades have two small pins running through the blade at each end. These pins fit slots on rotating holders, at each end of the U, and attach the blade to the saw body. The holders have a short arm, shaped somewhat like half a wing nut. By rotating these arms together, the blade can be adjusted to different angles. Because the blade is thin, it can easily be broken by twisting one end and not the other. To remove a blade, hold the short arm nearest the handle, so the blade won't twist, and unscrew the handle. Unscrewing the handle releases the tension on the blade and allows the pins on the blade to slide out of the slots in the holders *(Figure 19)*.

To install a new blade, first loosen the handle as far as it will go without coming apart. Position the blade with the points of the teeth pointing back towards the handle so the saw will cut on the backstroke. Then put the pegs of the saw blade into the holder slots on the saw. Tighten the handle with one hand and keep the blade from twisting with the other.

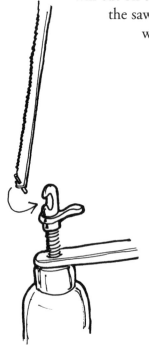

Figure 19.
To change a coping saw blade, unscrew the handle until the blade will slide out of its holder.

How to Use the Coping Saw

A coping saw requires a light touch. Watch the blade. If it bends more than a little, too much pressure is being applied. The saw motion should be gently back and forth. As with other saws, it is the saw teeth moving through the wood, not the downward pressure, that cuts the wood. Sometimes kids mistakenly push down so hard they can barely move the saw back and forth. It is not uncommon to break a blade or two while learning.

In addition to the back and forth motion, the blade should be square (90 degrees) to the cut. Because kids don't quite understand what "square" or "90 degrees to" means, I give them a one inch square of wood to hold alongside the blade next to the cut and tell them to try to keep the blade parallel to the edge of the block of wood *(Figure 20)*.

Beginners have a tendency to try to turn the saw too quickly. Turning must be done gradually as the saw is moving back and forth. Pressure, angles, and motion make it a difficult saw for anyone to use. I don't introduce it till the second grade, but I'll let anyone who asks give it a try.

That said, a few kids will learn to use it with great dexterity. Motivation is the key. If a child really wants something that requires a curve, she can usually learn to use the coping saw. The routine is: practice, help, practice, help until the child acquires the skill. If she gets frustrated, suggest trying something else for a while.

Figure 20.
Kids have trouble keeping the blade of the coping saw square to the work. A trick that helps is to stop cutting for a second and hold a small square block of wood tight against the work, right up next to the blade. The blade should be parallel to the side of the block.

A coping saw can also be used to remove a piece of wood (a circle, for example) from the center of a board without cutting in from the edge. To do this, first drill a hole through the circle. Remove the saw blade from the saw and put it through the hole in the circle. Re-attach the blade to the saw. Cut out the circle—which will entail changing the blade angle—and then remove the blade so the saw can be separated from the wood *(Figure 21)*.

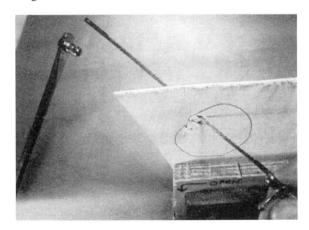

Figure 21.
To cut a large hole in a piece of wood without cutting through the edge, disconnect the coping saw blade and push it through a small hole (that you previously drilled) in the wood. Then reconnect the blade and cut out the big hole. The picture shows the blade ready to be reattached to the coping saw.

DRILLS

When kids can drill holes, they can build a wider variety of projects. A thin slice of tree branch can be turned into a key ring with a hole and some string. By drilling holes in one end, a thicker slice of the same branch can be transformed into a pencil holder for Mom or Dad. Drilling holes allows kids to use screws, which make stronger projects. Drilling holes for nails helps emphasize getting the nails in the correct place so projects go together with less frustration.

As a safety reminder, the biggest safety concern is not from using a drill but from accidentally poking someone while transporting it or while changing bits. The bit should not be pointed at any body parts. Use it or put it down.

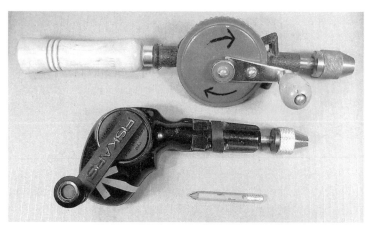

Figure 22.
*The hand drill is on top
with the Fiskars below it.*

The following paragraphs will describe five drills you can use with children. One drill is enough to start small groups, but an extra drill (or two) means bits won't have to be changed as frequently. Start with the hand drill, the Fiskars, or the spiral screwdriver. The hand drill and the Fiskars drill are very similar and operate in the same manner. These two drills work well for holes up to $5/16$". The spiral screwdriver, as its name implies, is used to put in screws but can also be used to drill holes. It will not drill holes as large or as deep as either the Fiskars or the hand drill but it is useful for small holes, and children enjoy mastering the up and down motion. Two friends recently told me the spiral screwdriver was their favorite childhood tool.

For projects that require larger holes (the stool), there are two choices: the brace and bit or the hand-operated drill press. The brace and bit is much easier to find (available at good hardware stores) but it is difficult for children to use. I'll wait until children are six or so to try it and then supervise them closely. For younger children, I'll hold the brace and let the child turn the handle.

Although a small hand-operated drill press is difficult to find (look on the internet under "antique tools" or "hand-operated drill press"), it makes a great addition to any kids' shop class.

The Hand Drill and the Fiskars Drill

You've probably seen the typical hand drill: it looks a bit like an egg beater. The Fiskars is smaller. The gears are enclosed but it works in the same way. One hand holds the drill upright and the other rotates the handle clockwise which turns the bit. The Fiskars may be a little easier for younger kids to use but the hand drill will make a slightly larger hole. Both drills are shown in *Figure 22.*

Changing Bits

The part of the drill that holds the bit is called the chuck. The chuck can be opened or closed to fit different sized bits. To remove a bit and replace it with another one, first open the chuck by holding it tight with one hand and turn the drill handle counterclockwise with the other hand. Drilling holes tightens the bit, so you may need to jerk or hit the handle (while you grasp the chuck) to break the bit loose.

Once the bit is loose, the jaws of the chuck may be opened or closed by rotating the chuck, still holding the handle tight. Place the desired bit in the chuck, hold the chuck tight with one hand, and turn the handle clockwise as tight as you can. If, when using the drill, the bit stops and the chuck slips around it, the bit is not tight enough. Re-tighten it.

Using the Hand Drill and the Fiskars Drill

The first step of drilling is to hold the wood so it can't move. If you are working on a small piece of wood, put it in the vice. A larger piece can be clamped to the workbench or held on the floor with the knee as you lean over the drill. Protect the floor with a piece of scrap wood.

Both drills can be used horizontally or vertically, whichever is easier for the particular child. Try the horizontal position first. It is easier for most children and safer, too. In the horizontal position, a child can hold the top of the drill steady against her body and lean into it.

Using the drill in the vertical position will work better for some. The drawback to this position is that children let go of the drill and leave it hanging precariously on the bit when they want a rest. Bits get broken this way, but more importantly, the drill could fall to the floor, hitting someone on the way down.

In order for the bit to cut, the drill handle must be turned in the correct direction. Lefties are particularly prone to turning the wrong way. Painting an arrow on the handle acts as a reminder, but kids forget to look at it. I use the reminder "wrong way" frequently. The bit also tends to work loose from the chuck if rotated backwards.

To make things more complicated, the operator must push down with just the right amount of pressure. Not enough pressure and the bit doesn't cut; too much and it stops.

A common mistake is to push down so hard the bit is difficult to rotate. A drill bit does not push through the wood (or steel, or plastic). It cuts a little with each rotation. The bit must be kept moving to cut. It must be sharp, too; dull bits don't cut.

After the hole is finished, the bit still has to be removed from the wood. Often it does not come out easily. The natural inclination, to pull hard, could send the drill flying. The trick is to keep the bit rotating forward just like you are still drilling the hole, and gently pull the drill back (or lift the drill up). Kids want to reverse the direction of the drill and this works, too, but has the disadvantage of loosening the bit in the chuck.

The best way to help a young child develop competence with the drill is to sit down (I spend a lot of time sitting on a stool so I can be at a child's level) with her and help drill several holes in a row. For the first hole or two, I'll hold the drill straight and do most of the pushing down while she turns the handle. On subsequent holes, I'll gradually relinquish my role.

The Spiral Screwdriver (also a drill)

The spiral screwdriver *(Figure 23)*, which can also be used as a drill, rotates as the handle is pushed down. It is a great tool for drilling small holes in thin wood or for kids to practice taking screws in and out. Spiral screwdrivers used to be inexpensive. Now, unfortunately, everybody buys

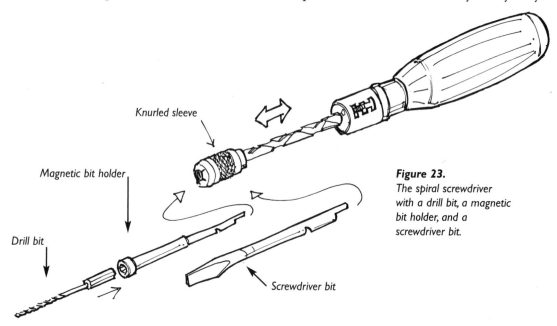

Knurled sleeve

Magnetic bit holder

Drill bit

Figure 23.
The spiral screwdriver with a drill bit, a magnetic bit holder, and a screwdriver bit.

Screwdriver bit

battery drills, so not many of these nifty little screwdrivers are made. Consequently, they're expensive, about $60.00. Keep an eye out at garage sales. I just found two great used spiral screwdrivers for $4.00.

The spiral screwdriver comes with an assortment of bits for drilling small holes or for driving screws. Often these are kept in the handle of the drill so it's easy to make a mini-lesson of choosing the correct bit. Extra spiral screwdriver bits can be purchased at a good hardware store. Alternatively, you can buy a special magnetic bit holder to fit the spiral screwdriver and then use standard hex bits in it. A small three-position switch selects forward, for putting screws in, reverse for removing screws, or center, which locks the bit to the handle so the spiral screwdriver can be used like a regular screwdriver. Beginners hold the spiral screwdriver vertically. An occasional drop of oil will keep the mechanical parts moving smoothly.

Changing Spiral Screwdriver Bits

First, be sure you're wearing eye protection before changing bits. To change bits *(Figure 24)*, hold the handle of the spiral screwdriver against your stomach with the bit pointing away from your (and anyone else's) body. In this position, if the bit comes out unexpectedly, you won't poke yourself. With the other hand, grasp the knurled sleeve (near the bit) and pull it back towards your body. After the drive mechanism is compressed, the sleeve will slip back about 1/8" and release the bit. It may take some wiggling. If the bit doesn't release, the sleeve is probably not back far enough or may need a drop of oil. Reverse this procedure to install the new bit. Upper elementary kids can learn to change bits properly, but supervise them closely. The point of compressing the tool against the stomach is to avoid compressing it against the workbench where it could spring up toward a child's face.

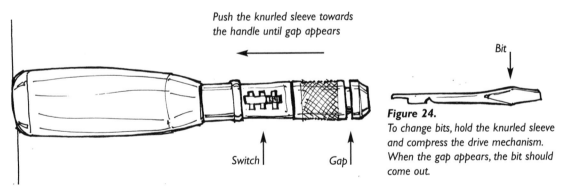

Push the knurled sleeve towards
the handle until gap appears

Bit

Switch   Gap

Figure 24.
To change bits, hold the knurled sleeve
and compress the drive mechanism.
When the gap appears, the bit should
come out.

Using the Spiral Screwdriver

To use the spiral screwdriver, first install the proper bit. Place the wood in the vice. Put the spiral screwdriver over the prospective hole. Grasp the knurled sleeve between the thumb and the forefinger of one hand, and move the drill handle up and down with the other hand. It is a tricky operation and requires practice. The bit has a tendency to lift as the handle goes up. The thumb and finger need to hold the bit down in the hole, counteracting the up movement of the other hand.

After the hole is finished, the bit must still be removed from the hole. This can be frustrating. Beginners intuitively pull up and, since it is hard to pull straight up, the bit binds and sticks. The trick is to turn the spiral screwdriver clockwise as if it were a regular screwdriver, and pull up at the same time.

The Brace

Before the advent of hand-held electric drills and the newer battery-powered drills, the brace *(Figure 25)* was the tool of choice for drilling larger holes and putting in or removing large screws. It's a good tool for kids but tricky to use because it is hard to hold the top of the brace steady, push down with the right amount of force, and rotate the handle all at the same time. Adjusting the ratcheting mechanism can be confusing, too.

The larger a hole, the harder it is to drill. Even $1/4"$ to $5/16"$ holes can be hard for younger children using the hand drill. With a brace, more downward pressure and leverage can be applied and the $3/8"$ holes for the pencil holder can be drilled without much trouble. Older kids may be able to use the brace for even larger holes.

A brace can also be used with a screwdriver bit to put in or take out screws. For the step stool project, which has eight screws, I have kids put the screws in about halfway with a screwdriver and then switch to the brace for the last half. It's a lot easier. The brace takes practice, but in any small group there will be someone who gets the hang of it. For adults, a brace with a screwdriver bit is a handy tool for driving and removing screws in projects like the workbench, miter block, or shelves, especially if you don't have a battery-operated drill.

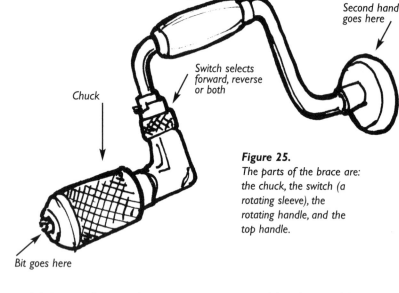

Rotating handle

Second hand goes here

Switch selects forward, reverse or both

Chuck

Bit goes here

Figure 25.
The parts of the brace are: the chuck, the switch (a rotating sleeve), the rotating handle, and the top handle.

Ratchet Mechanism

The brace has a ratchet mechanism *(Figure 26)* which allows it to rotate even if the handle is not turned in a full circle. A three-position switch, just above the chuck, determines whether the bit will turn in a complete circle as the handle turns, or whether it will ratchet in one direction or the other. The three switch positions each have corresponding bit movements:

1. In the middle position the handle does not ratchet and the bit turns the same direction as the handle. Occasionally, if not much time for explanations is available, I'll tape the ratchet mechanism in the center position so it won't be bumped to another position and cause confusion, but it is better to explain what the switch is and how it works.

2. Turn the switch clockwise and a brace and bit will drive a screw in clockwise, yet the handle does not have to turn in a full circle; it can be ratcheted backwards (counterclockwise) through any part of a turn. For adults, ratcheting backwards is handy (and necessary) if you're trying to drive a screw up next to a wall where the brace cannot be

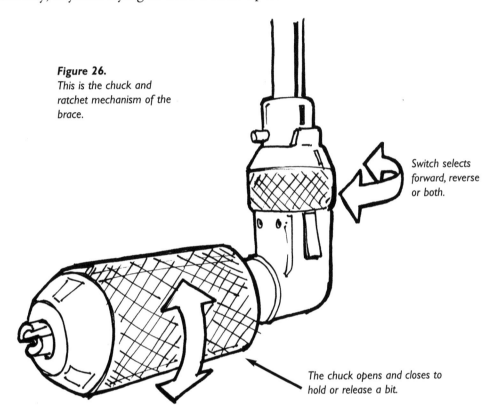

Figure 26.
This is the chuck and ratchet mechanism of the brace.

Switch selects forward, reverse or both.

The chuck opens and closes to hold or release a bit.

turned in a complete circle. For kids, ratcheting backwards part way through a rotation makes it easier to keep the top of the brace steady. When driving screws, ratcheting helps keep the bit from popping out of the screw.

3. The third position, turning the sleeve counterclockwise, lets the brace turn counterclockwise to remove screws while ratcheting clockwise through any part of a turn. If the sleeve is accidentally bumped into this position, the bit won't rotate in the proper direction for cutting and an inexperienced person might think the brace was broken.

Changing Bits

Installing a bit in the brace is similar to installing a bit in a hand drill: open the chuck, put the bit into it, and then close the chuck. To keep the chuck from ratcheting, put the sleeve that controls the ratchet mechanism in the middle position. Hold the chuck tight and turn the crank handle counterclockwise to open. Put a bit in the chuck and turn the handle clockwise to close the chuck around the bit as tight as you can get it.

Using the Brace to Drill Holes

I think the easiest position for using the brace is on the floor with the child bent over the top of the brace *(Figure 27)*. To drill large holes (3/8" for the pencil holder, for example), first install the appropriate bit. I find for holes up to 1/2" the twist drill bits cut faster than do the flat spade bits. Set the ratchet mechanism in the middle position (explained above). The brace requires lots of downward pressure for the bit to cut.

If the piece is small, hold it with a clamp so it won't spin. A larger piece can be kept from moving, if necessary, with your knee. Place the object in a safe and out-of-the-way place on the floor. The left hand goes on the top round handle and the right hand goes on the turning handle—opposite for lefties. Have the child lean over the top of the brace with his chest or stomach, whichever is comfortable, on the hand which is on the upper knob. Turn the handle clockwise. The pressure applied to the brace will control how fast it cuts. Not enough and it won't cut; too much and it becomes hard to turn. Two kids can work together, one holding the brace upright and pressing down and the other turning the brace. Another way that works for some kids is to position the object to be drilled in the vice so that the brace and the hole are horizontal. This way the child can lean into the brace to provide the necessary pressure. If a younger child can't make headway by himself, I'll often hold the brace in this horizontal position while he turns the crank handle. I find holding the brace and the object in the vice vertically doesn't work too well because children are too short to provide much downward pressure and turn the drill at the same time. In this vertical position, children tire easily and sometimes let go of the brace, leaving it hanging on the bit. This is a dangerous situation as the brace can easily fall to the floor, hitting someone on the way down.

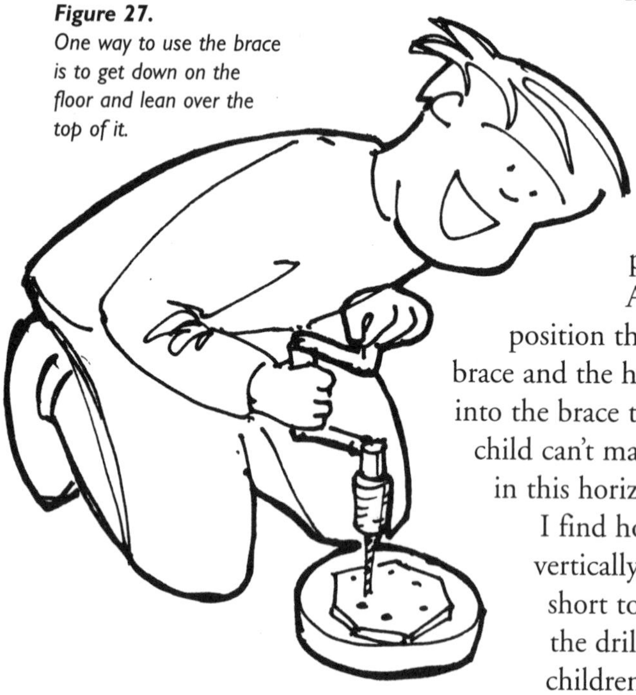

Figure 27.
One way to use the brace is to get down on the floor and lean over the top of it.

Using the Brace to Drive or Remove Screws

To use the brace to drive or remove screws, place a magnetic bit holder in the chuck and put the appropriate screwdriver bit in the holder. The magnetic bit holder allows bits to be changed quickly without opening and closing the chuck. Holding and turning the brace for screws is the same as for drilling holes. Setting up the project is a bit different.

Place the object to be worked on in the vice or, if it's too big, hold it down with a knee or clamp and work on the floor. Set the ratchet mechanism in the forward position so the brace doesn't have to be turned in a complete circle. Start the screws by putting them in about halfway through the first board with a screwdriver. Have a helper hold the two pieces together in position. Hold the brace over the screw as if you're drilling a hole and rotate clockwise while pressing down. Make sure the screw actually turns. If the brace isn't held down hard enough, the bit will just slip in the screw head.

A brace will remove extremely tight screws. For example, if you need to move a vice held to the workbench with screws that cannot be removed with a screwdriver, try a brace. The most common mistake is not to push down hard enough to hold the bit tight in the screw slot. This results in chewed up bits and screws. Tricks for removing screws include having the appropriate bit for the screw, using the brace before the screw heads are chewed up, pushing down hard (really hard) so the bit won't slip, and jerking the brace handle by hitting it to jar the screw loose.

The Hand-Operated Drill Press

I found a hand-operated drill press *(Figure 28)* at an antique tool sale. It makes many drilling operations easier and safer. With it, a child doesn't have to support the weight of the drill or hold it straight. The feed mechanism allows her to apply more pressure to the bit. Kids enjoy using it.

Many types of hand-operated drill presses were made in the early 1900s. The more complicated and sophisticated ones, with a flywheel and automatic feed mechanisms, are not appropriate for children. Mine is basically a big hand drill, held in a stand, with a screw mechanism to raise or lower the bit. Mount it on a bench 12" high so the handle will be at about shoulder level for a child.

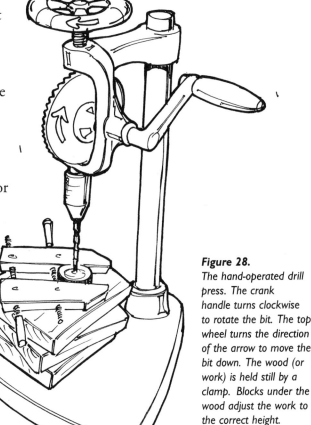

Figure 28.
The hand-operated drill press. The crank handle turns clockwise to rotate the bit. The top wheel turns the direction of the arrow to move the bit down. The wood (or work) is held still by a clamp. Blocks under the wood adjust the work to the correct height.

Using the Drill Press

Install the proper bit in the same way as for the hand drill. Get the wood ready to be drilled by raising the bit up as far as it will go and blocking up underneath the wood, if necessary, to get it up close to the bit. Hold the wood so it won't move. Small pieces can be clamped as shown in *Figure 28*. Large wood will spin a half turn or so until it hits the pipe that supports the drill and stops. Now you're ready to begin the actual drilling.

Using the drill press is a little like rubbing your stomach and patting your head. There are two controls, one for each hand, and they have different motions. A handle on the right, like the one on the hand drill, rotates the drill bit. A wheel on top of the drill press moves the bit either up or down. To drill a hole, both controls need to be turned clockwise at the same time. The right hand needs to keep the drill turning at a comfortable speed while the left hand feeds the bit into the wood at the appropriate rate—slow for large holes and faster for smaller ones. Both wheels should be marked with a clockwise pointing arrow as a reminder of the correct direction to turn. Nearly everyone turns the top wheel down too fast, which jams the bit into the wood and stops it from rotating.

Teaching kids how to use this tool is a classic example of words not really helping much. At first I would tell a child to slow the top wheel but they just didn't hear it. A better approach is to pace them with a little chant, "one, two, quarter turn." This means turn the crank handle once around, twice around, and then turn the down feed (top wheel) a

Figure 29.
Kelsey and Jillian working together on the drill press.

quarter turn. If a child still has trouble, I'll suggest he put his left hand behind his back and use one hand for both operations. The same little chant sometimes helps here, too. It takes practice and often I'll have to come back and help 3 or 4 times. Two children can work together, if they communicate, one operating the down feed and the other rotating the bit *(Figure 29)*. After the hole is finished, the bit must still be removed from the hole. First raise the wood up (by turning the up-down wheel counterclockwise) until there is plenty of room underneath it. Then rotate the drill (same direction as for drilling) and push down on the wood at the same time.

About Drill Bits

Drill bits can be purchased in a set or separately. A set is cheaper and comes in a handy box arranged by size. A small set from $1/8$" to $3/8$" in $1/16$" increments is a good start. Be sure the $3/8$" and $5/16$" bits have a $1/4$" shank (the part that fits in the drill) because many hand drills and the Fiskars won't accept anything larger than $1/4$". Children tend to bend or break bits smaller than $1/8$" so I use nails with the heads cut off as bits for those smaller sizes. Nails don't drill as well as bits but they work well enough for small sizes and are easy to replace.

For the brace, I use twist drill bits for sizes between $1/4$" to $1/2$". Twist bits don't quite fit properly into the brace but will work for small sizes and cut faster at the slow speeds at which children turn the brace. For the few larger holes ($3/4$" for the camping stool, for example) use either auger or spade bits. A good sharp auger bit will cut faster than the newer flat spade bits, but they are more expensive. A dull spade bit can be quite frustrating for a child. *Figure 30* shows a twist drill bit, a spade bit and an auger bit.

It is important to choose the correct size bit for each job. A hole to fit a dowel that is to be the mast of a model boat, for example, must be the same size as the dowel. A pilot hole for a screw (or nail) must be smaller than the screw, or the fastener will not hold. Unless kids have been shown how to choose an appropriate bit, they often use whatever bit is handy, with predictable results.

Drill bits and dowels are labeled so sizes can be matched from the labels, assuming the labels aren't worn off. Many round objects are standard sizes, so if a dowel and drill bit look close in size there is a good chance they are the same. Check by holding the dowel (or round object) and bit side by side, and then

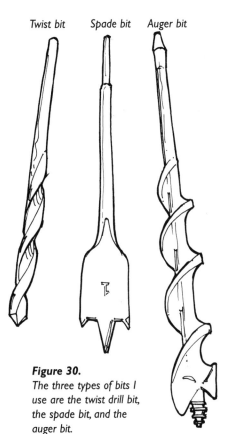

Twist bit　　Spade bit　　Auger bit

Figure 30.
The three types of bits I use are the twist drill bit, the spade bit, and the auger bit.

look down at the ends to compare diameters. It is amazing how even an untrained eye can tell if two objects are the same, or nearly so, in size *(Figure 31)*. If you are still not sure, drill a test hole in a piece of scrap before risking the real thing.

Another method is to teach kids to measure the dowel (or other round object) and bit with inexpensive plastic calipers. Slide the dowel between the caliper jaws. Rotate it. The dowel should

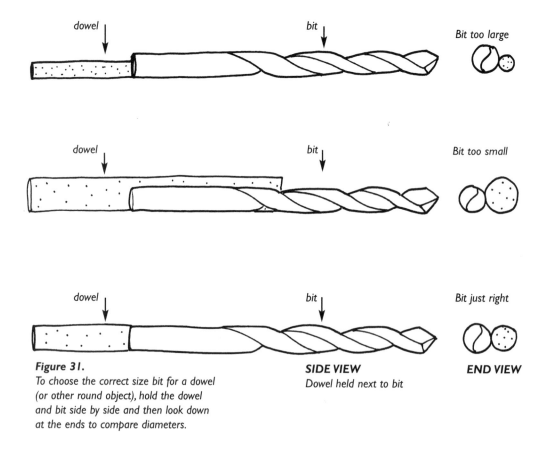

Figure 31.
To choose the correct size bit for a dowel (or other round object), hold the dowel and bit side by side and then look down at the ends to compare diameters.

SIDE VIEW
Dowel held next to bit

END VIEW

barely touch the calipers. Remove the dowel and replace it with the drill bit. If the bit is too large, it won't fit without forcing the caliper jaws apart. If the bit is too small, there will be a little play between the caliper jaws and the bit. The correct bit will have the same fit as the dowel. Upper elementary kids can learn to use the calipers and choose their own bits, but I do it for younger students.

For drilling nail pilot holes, choose a bit (or nail used as a bit) just a little smaller than the nail to be used. Test on two pieces of scrap by drilling, nailing and then trying to pull apart. If they come apart easily, the pilot hole is too large. If the wood splits as the nail is driven, the pilot hole is too small.

The proper sized hole for non-tapered screws (like sheetrock screws) is the diameter of the shank. Or to say it another way, the hole should be the size of the screw without threads. Hold a bit alongside the screw. Looking past the bit at the screw, the correct size bit will block out the shank but not the threads *(Figure 32)*. Too large a hole doesn't allow the threads to catch and hold.

Bits need to be sharp. You can tell if a bit is dull by looking carefully at the cutting edge. A dull cutting edge will reflect light and appear as a bright spot, just like a dull saw. Good quality twist bits used only on wood will stay sharp for a long time. Unless you know how or can get a lesson from an old-timer or machinist, it's probably better to buy new twist bits than to resharpen them yourself.

Figure 32.
The screw shank should be the same diameter as the bit. The threads should stick out beyond the bit.

A spade bit gets dull faster than a twist bit, but can be re-sharpened with a file. Look for the bright spot that reveals a dull cutting edge and file it down, trying to follow the original angle. Auger bits can be sharpened, too, but you'll need a lesson from someone who knows how to do it.

HAMMERS

I've tried quite a few different weight hammers with kids: 7 ounce, 13 ounce, 16 ounce, and 22 ounce. Eventually I concluded the 7 ounce was too light and the 22 ounce a bit heavy. The tendency of a child is to choke up on the hammer handle and to take short strokes. With the 7 ounce hammer, not much energy actually hits the nail. More energy actually gets to the nail from a bigger hammer and a longer stroke. A 13 to 16 ounce hammer is ideal for preschool and early elementary children. For bigger nails or older children, a 22 ounce hammer might work better.

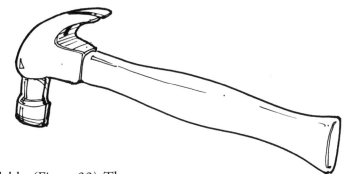

CLAMPS

It is a good idea to have a few clamps available *(Figure 33)*. They can act as very strong extra hands. For my summer class, I have two 3" clamps, two 4" clamps and one wooden clamp which opens to 6". The smaller clamps can be used to clamp pieces of wood to the workbench while they are being sawn, drilled, or sanded, or they can hold wood in the miter block. The bigger clamps are useful for holding larger pieces of wood to the workbench or to a stool so they can be cut. When using clamps, the most common mistake children make is to turn the clamp the wrong direction. Many's the time I've see a child attempting to clamp a piece of wood in the miter block only to be opening the clamp instead of closing it. It's clockwise (looking down on top of the clamp) to tighten, but many kids don't understand clockwise. The only foolproof way for kids to know if the clamp is opening or closing is to watch it and see. I tell kids, "Get it straight in your mind what you want the clamp to do, open or close. Then turn the handle and see if the clamp is doing what you want it to. If it isn't, turn the handle the other way."

The above advice helps when tightening the clamp but when the clamp is already tight, it is easy to forget which direction will loosen it. I draw little pictures saying "open" with an arrow going in a counterclockwise direction and "close" with an arrow going in a clockwise direction on the workbench, miter box, and vices to act as reminders.

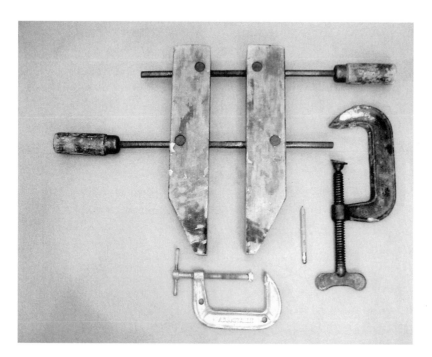

Figure 33.
Clamps are a helpful shop tool. Kids can usually learn to handle a C-clamp. The other clamp, with two handles and two parallel clamping surfaces, can be confusing.

To use a clamp, first open it slightly more than the pieces being clamped. Hold the pieces being clamped in position, position the clamp, and then tighten the clamp the final few turns. When removing the clamp, it is only necessary to loosen it a turn or two. Often kids loosen the clamp an inch (or more) instead of just a couple of turns. If they are making repeat cuts, this means taking up the inch before using the clamp again. One or two turns each direction saves time and frustration.

THE SQUARE

Once children start building a specific project I tell them, "Building is like making pieces of a puzzle; unless the pieces are the correct shape, they won't fit together." Probably the most important shape for beginning woodworkers is what's called square, or 90 degrees. The corners of a box will meet if each board is cut square to the edge. Shelves will fit inside a bookcase if the ends are square. The stern of a toy boat will look better if it is square to the centerline of the boat. To make these square cuts, you can use a tool called a square to make an edge against which you can draw a pencil line. *Figure 34* shows a traditional square and a try square.

Figure 34.
The top picture is a traditional square. Below it is a try square which can also be used for drawing 45 degree angles.

A square has a thin blade offset exactly 90 degrees to a thicker handle. If the thick part of the square is held tightly against a straight edge of a board, the thin edge will mark a square cut across the board. Children often make the mistake of not holding the thicker handle of the square tightly against the board edge. They understand the idea of using a straight edge to draw a straight line, but often miss that a straight line isn't necessarily square *(Figure 35).*

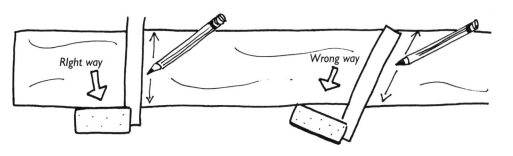

Right way

Wrong way

Figure 35.
To draw a line square to the edge of a board, the fat part of the square must be tight up against the board.

SURFORM PLANES

Surform planes *(Figure 36)* are more like a rasp or super coarse sandpaper than like a traditional woodworking plane. They are safe because instead of one big sharp blade like traditional planes, they have a blade with many small cutting surfaces. These blades can be replaced after they become dull.

Figure 36.
Two types of Surform planes.

A Surform plane is used for shaping and/or removing small amounts of wood from a project. For example, a child might want to round the corners of a project to make it look more finished. Another common use for the Surform is to smooth up rough or crooked saw cuts. While sandpaper would work for both of these operations, a Surform removes wood faster and easier.

I use two different shaped Surforms with kids. One is flat and about 6" long. To use this plane, put the project wood in the vice. Hold the plane on top of the wood and push it away from your body along the surface of the wood. Lift the plane up, bring it back and repeat the same motion over and over. When you install a new blade on the 6" plane, make sure it cuts as you push the plane away.

The second Surform has a shorter curved blade which can reach into small spaces or conform to curves the 6" Surform glides over. This Surform works best when the blade is installed so it cuts on the pull stroke. The project wood should be in a vice before using this small Surform, too.

COUNTERSINK AND NAIL SET

Sometimes it's a good idea to sink fastenings below the surface of the wood. It looks better, and if fastenings are on the bottom of a project, sinking them protects any surface (the dining room table, for example) the project might be placed on. This is called countersinking.

For screws, the tool used is called a countersink *(Figure 37,* black handle). It works like a drill bit by rotating, thus making a larger hole for the screw head to fit into. Countersinks that fit into a drill are also available, but I find it handy to have a separate tool, as it reduces the number of bit changes. The two screws on the bottom of the flipper project are an example of when countersinking should be done.

To countersink nails, the tool to use is a nail set, the smaller tool shown in *Figure 37*. To use the nail set, hold it on the nail head and hit it with a hammer, driving the nail below the surface of the wood *(Figure 38)*. The nails holding the bottom of a box, for example, should be countersunk.

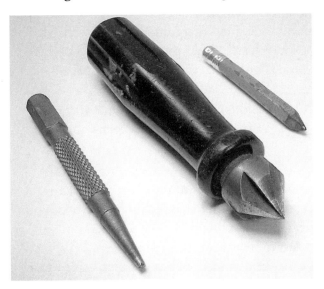

Figure 37.
The nail set and the countersink.

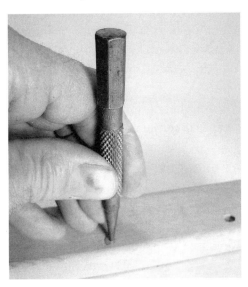

Figure 38.
The nail set ready to be hit with a hammer.

SANDPAPER AND SANDING

When my son Andrew was 16 and doing his annual spring cleaning, under a heap of clothes and sailing gear he unearthed a beautiful piece of bird's-eye maple he had sanded smooth when he was in kindergarten. For years, he kept it on his shelf just to look at or handle from time to time. This reminded me how much children appreciate sanding a piece of wood and turning it into an object of beauty.

Sandpaper comes in different grits. The lower the grit number, the coarser the paper. Thirty-six grit paper is very coarse. It literally shreds wood. I use it for taking paint off boats or houses, but I can't think of an occasion when children would need it. Eighty grit is a medium paper (the one I use most with children) used to smooth up the rough edges of wood and get rid of splinters. If a finer finish is desired, 220 grit can produce a nearly mirror-like finish.

Buying Sandpaper

Sheet sandpaper is expensive. It seems like the price (but not quality) goes up every year. Sheet paper doesn't seem to last long, either. I get around this by buying 6" X 48" sanding belts and cutting them up. Because belts are industrial quality and designed to be run on machines hour after hour, they last much longer than sheet paper and, in the end, cost considerably less.

To give you an idea about how long sanding belts will last, I buy two 6" X 48" industrial sanding belts at the beginning of my summer class and cut them into 6" or 8" sections. The class serves 60 kids and the sandpaper gets a lot of hard use. At the end of six weeks there might be a little left, but not much. I'll also use about 5 sheets of 220 wet-dry paper, cut it into $1/8$s, and pass it out to dedicated sanders.

Another option is to buy a pack (100 4" X 11" sheets) of sheetrock sandpaper. This paper is considerably cheaper than regular sheet sandpaper and about the same quality.

Sandpaper Setup

An easy way to sand small (but not large) pieces of wood is to move the wood across a stationary piece of sandpaper. This works considerably better than holding the wood in one hand and sandpaper in the other. To set this up, cut sanding belts into 6" pieces and hot glue the sandpaper to a board. Fasten the board to the workbench with screws.

Larger pieces of wood should be held in a vice and sanded with sandpaper stapled to a small block of wood. Another sanding trick is to cut small pieces of sandpaper and glue them to various dowels and small sticks to get into those places that are hard to reach with regular sandpaper.

Sanding to Remove Slivers

Slivers are a part of woodworking, but a good sanding job will reduce them to a minimum. I try to instill that it is a builder's responsibility to make a project as safe as possible, which includes removing all the slivers. Try to get the kids to sand each saw cut and then give the finished project a final sand.

Sanding for a Fine Finish

The first rule of sanding is to try to sand with the grain of the wood. Sanding across the grain leaves scratches. When sanding something round, it's difficult to follow this rule, so don't worry about it. The cross-grain scratches will come out as you move to finer paper.

The ideal way to sand to a fine finish is to work through the sandpaper grits. If the surface is rough, start with 60 grit paper. Sand until all the big scratches and grooves are gone. Then move to finer paper, say, 120 grit. Sand until all the scratches from the coarser paper are gone and are replaced with marks of the finer paper. Then go to finer paper still, say 220, and sand till all the scratches from the 120 paper are gone. 220 will produce a nice finish.

Most children, especially the younger ones, have a hard time understanding it's easier to sand away the larger scratches with coarse paper. If there are three different grits of paper available, children will want to move to the finest grit right away, which makes removing big scratches more difficult. My compromise is to use 80 grit for everything except when a child shows special interest in sanding and then I'll give him his own special piece of 220 paper. Out of ten kids, at least one or two work hard at sanding. Every once in a while, there will be an obsessive sander and for him I'll get out the 400 grit paper, the rubbing compound (like super fine sandpaper) and wax for a final polish.

Dull Sandpaper

The other day a friend asked how to tell if sandpaper is working. The answer is, by feeling a new piece alongside a worn piece. New paper will feel sharp; old paper will feel smoother. Half-worn paper will feel, well, about half-worn. Just as a sharp saw saves a lot of work, so does sharp sandpaper. Check it frequently. It's not uncommon to see novices happily sanding away with a smooth sheet of paper, accomplishing very little.

HOMEMADE MITER BLOCK

Sometimes the successful completion of a project depends on the ability to make straight cuts. The four sides of a box, for example, must be straight or the box won't fit together. The same with small furniture. If the cuts aren't straight, the pieces of the table, chair, or bed may not fit together. With practice, most kindergartners can learn to make straight cuts, but a miter block makes the job easier, makes the results more consistent, and allows children as young as three or four to be successful. This homemade miter block *(Figure 39)* is easy to use and will hold different sizes of wood. Older kids make these to use at home. See the Appendix, page 187 for constructions details.

Figure 39.
The miter block is made from two short pieces of 4 X 4. These 4 X 4s are mounted on a piece of plywood and separated by a saw cut. The wood to be cut is placed in the corner tight against the 4X4. Younger children can use a clamp to hold the wood tight. Older kids, if they can keep the wood from moving, can skip the clamp and hold the wood in place by hand.

THE HOT GLUE GUN

Of all the tools I've used with kids, the hot glue gun is responsible for more creativity, serious messing about, and fun than any other single tool *(Figure 40)*. The magic of the hot glue is that it dries fast and therefore allows small pieces of all kinds of materials to be fastened together quickly in a myriad of ways. With hot glue, kids will create the most amazing array of sculpture from coffee stir sticks, film canisters, small scraps of wood, nuts, bolts, screws, gears, and small parts from old VCRs. Hot glue also provides a quick way to assemble more practical projects like small boxes, tiny furniture, airplanes, and rafts, to name just a few. w

Figure 40.
Samantha and Kylie at the glue gun station at the Childlife Montessori School, Fall 2004.

Use the small low-temperature glue guns and glue only. Guns and glue sticks will both be marked "low-temp." The bigger guns that operate at higher temperatures can cause serious burns. **Do not use them.** Place cardboard or thin plywood on the workspace top to protect it from little globs of spilled glue. Set up an out-of-the-way workspace. Provide one glue gun for each beginner. Two experienced children can share a glue gun, but may need to be reminded about sharing. Make a place for the glue gun halfway between two work stations by tracing around it with a felt pen. Teach children to put the gun in this outline when they are finished gluing, thinking about the next step, or looking for the next piece to glue.

Before students use the hot glue gun, I give them the hot glue speech, which goes like this: "Hot glue is HOT and if you get it on your finger, it will burn you. The metal tip of the gun is also very hot. Don't touch it. Keep your fingers out of the glue. If you accidentally get glue on your finger, wipe it off quickly and you will not get burned. If you do get burned, it does hurt but not for long and you'll probably survive. If you don't feel comfortable using the glue gun, I'd be happy to do it for you." I keep ice around just in case. I demonstrate how to avoid burns by putting glue on my finger and quickly wiping it off. Most kids learn quickly how not to burn themselves. Cause and effect is a good teacher. An occasional child doesn't seem to learn and keeps sticking his finger into the glue. I encourage these kids to find something else to do.

Glue Gun Tips

- Demonstrate how glue sticks go into the back of the gun. Then explain that the glue melts inside and comes out the tip.
- Hot glue dries quickly. Apply glue to an inch or two of wood and then assemble. Using long runs of glue will result in the glue drying before pieces can be assembled.
- Hot glue is for small objects only. It won't hold larger pieces of wood together for any length of time; they must be nailed or screwed together. I mention this because occasionally kids get so carried away with the magic of hot glue they start reaching for the 2 X 4s.
- Hot glue is not waterproof. Bird houses or boats which are to be used in water are not good candidates for hot glue construction.

CHAPTER THREE·WOOD & MEASURING

WOOD

You can count on food being available at the grocery store, at prices similar to your last visit. It's different with wood. Price, kind, quality, and availability vary enormously from store to store, from one part of the country to another, from year to year, and even during different times of the year. If you need a particular type of wood tomorrow, count on it being hard to find and expensive.

On the other hand, if you tap into the wood subculture and collect it ahead of time, it's amazing how much wood, perfect for kids, is thrown away. Most of the wood I use comes free from sawmills, scrap bins, wood piles, and lumber yards. For years my best source was a local cedar sawmill. They had a huge scrap pile with short pieces which were actually better than anything I could buy. I selected the best pieces and spent an hour loading and then maybe four hours at home re-sawing. A short day's work provided most of the wood for a year's classes. Much to my dismay, the mill burned down. Now most of my wood comes from the scrap bin at a store that installs doors and from the leftovers of a friend's carving business.

Wood to Look For

- Small pieces of wood that are easy to cut and free or inexpensive. Here in the Pacific Northwest that means cedar, pine, birch, hemlock, spruce, and fir. Other areas of the country will have different kinds of wood. Talk to a local woodworker. Look for short 1 X 4s, 1 X 6s.

- 2 X 4s and 2 X 6s. The 1" and 2" material can be resawn into different sizes and thicknesses. Larger wood can be used, but takes more time to resaw into smaller pieces kids can handle.

- Branches 2"-3" in diameter make great pencil holders. Smaller diameter branches make key rings and wood collection pieces. Cedar, maple, and birch sand to a beautiful finish. Freshly cut branches need to be dried for several months so they won't develop cracks (checks). Cut branches into 3- or 4-foot lengths, paint the ends to slow drying, and store in a cool place.

- Round wood. Broom handles, dowels, and chair legs.

- Small weird-shaped pieces can be used for sculpture. Often cleaning up the scraps around a band saw will provide these. Ask at a cabinet shop or ask a parent with a band saw. Look for small pieces of a few hardwoods like oak, walnut, or ash for the more experienced kids. Avoid tropical hardwoods, as some are toxic.

- Thin pieces of wood from wine boxes or orange crates can be used to make small boxes and furniture.

- Cubes 3/4"-1", or odd shapes, and 1" diameter branches of different kinds of wood are good for wood sanding and key rings. A parent with a band saw could make these from larger scrap pieces.

- Small pieces of driftwood make great sculptures.

- Pressboard is particle board without the glue. It isn't very strong but is easy to cut and has a good finish for drawing. I use it for puzzles, a first coping saw project, because it is easier to cut than plywood.

Wood to Avoid

- Particle board or any treated lumber, because of glue and toxins.

- Plywood, except for a small amount, because it is hard to cut, sand, or plane. I sometimes use 1/4" or 3/8" plywood for puzzles, project bases, or where strength is needed, like on the bottom of the camping stool project.

- Hardwoods like oak and ash which, although beautiful, are hard for beginners to cut, drill, and shape. The exceptions are a box of small pieces for sanding (see wood sanding) and a few pieces for special projects.

- Dirty or painted lumber unless you know someone with a planer that has carbide blades to clean it up. Serious dirt or paint will dull ordinary planer blades quickly. It is also possible old paint will be lead-based so the dust from planing would be toxic. That said, my planer with carbide blades has allowed me to turn several thousand board feet of painted, dirty, and weathered lumber into useful projects.

- Pallets or packing crates, mostly. The wood in pallets or packing crates is usually of poor quality. Even if good wood ends up in a pallet, it's tricky to separate from the pallet without destroying it. There are exceptions, however. A woman in one of my workshops said all her wood came from pallets. She used a circular saw to cut short pieces between the frames to avoid pulling nails. Be careful if you try this, because it is tricky to cut the boards without pinching the saw blade.

- Boards with cracks, splits, lots of big knots, or rot.

Wood Sources

Lumber Yards

Lumber yards often have scrap piles containing the leftovers from custom jobs. Quality varies enormously. Take only what you can use. Don't be talked into taking the whole scrap barrel. You might have to visit more than once to find something good. On the other hand, if you get to know people who work at the lumber yard and let them know you need wood for kids, they might save the good scrap for you.

Your Neighborhood

Driving around the neighborhood, I might notice a construction site or someone trimming trees. Often I'll stop and ask if I can have some scrap pieces or a few branches for my kids' woodworking class. In a few minutes, I can get enough branches for pencil holders for a year or project wood for a month.

Woodworkers

Most wood shops have a scrap barrel. Much of this may not be useful for children, but some of it will be. In any group of 25 children, there will often be at least one parent or grandparent interested in woodworking. They can be of invaluable help in both finding and preparing wood for projects. Contact them through your newsletter or by asking any woodworker.

Cabinet Shops

Defective door casings, molding, and short cabinet trim are all good wood for kids. Several cabinet shops here in Bellingham leave scraps of trim, molding, and boards in the alley for free.

Small Sawmills

Mills that specialize in cutting fence boards or $3/4''$ lumber (around here, it is cedar mills) often have short pieces of leftover lumber that have to be disposed of. Much of it will be perfect for kids.

Construction or Remodeling Sites

Construction (and destruction) sites can be dangerous places. Get permission. Be careful of nails, loose boards, and falling objects. Often there will be an easily accessible scrap pile. Look for short 1 X 4s, 1 X 6s, 2 X 4s or 2 X 6s that can be resawn. Window or door trim, cedar siding, and shakes or shingles are also good.

Free

The free column of your local newspaper may have ads for free lumber. Most of this is not good but every once in a while there will be a real find. I once got 100 lightly stained cedar fence boards with very few nail holes.

The Recycling Store

In our town there is a store that sells recycled building materials. They have a free box and a $.10 box from which I have obtained materials. I suspect if I asked for wood for children's classes, a good deal would be forthcoming.

Buying Wood

Here in the Pacific Northwest, I have purchased low quality pine or cedar fence boards. Spring sales of these items are sometimes not too expensive and the quality is OK if you choose only the good boards from the pile. Recently, inexpensive spruce has appeared and I've used it. Compare stores, look for straight boards, smaller knots, finer grain, and no cracks. Avoid rotten boards. Don't be afraid to buy the good boards and leave the bad ones, but restack the pile carefully.

Wood Preparation

Resawing wood into smaller pieces is the most important preparation task. The table saw is the most useful wood preparation tool, but I also use my drill press for the spinning top project (page 70), my router to cut the blanks for the do-nothing-machine (page 142), and the band saw to cut out puzzle blanks or odd-shaped pieces for sculpture. If you do not have access to these tools or don't know how to use them, I encourage you to find a woodworker to prepare the wood for you. Another option is to contact a high school shop class. This prep work could be perfect for a student community service project. Additional preparation for specific projects may be required and will be covered in the directions for each project.

After you get wood, you can make it more useful by resawing it into strips *(Figure 41)* with a table saw. The thickness and width of the wood available will determine what the kids can build. Smaller wood is easy for young children to cut and it can be hot glued together, instead of nailed.

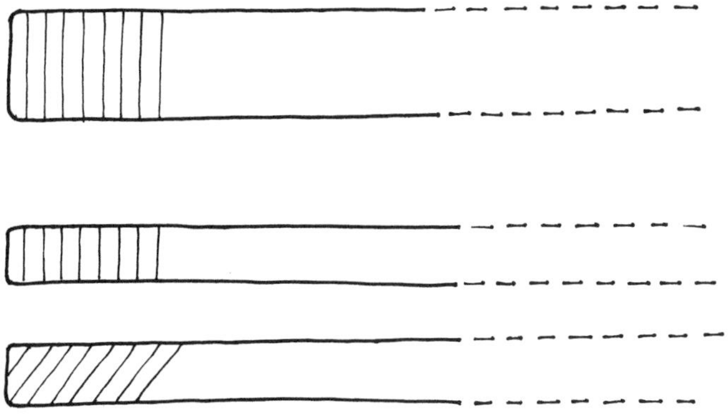

Figure 41.
Cutting standard lumber into strips provides more building opportunities for kids. Diagonal strips are for the marble roll project.

By cutting wood into strips, more projects can be built from any given piece. To illustrate, it is hard for a child to build much out of a two foot long 2 X 4, but if that same 2 X 4 is cut into 1/4" strips, she can make several small boxes, or quite a bit of small doll furniture, or use it for edging on bird feeders.

Most of the wood I use is from standard lumber. Two-inch lumber (which is actually only 1 1/2") comes in various widths: 2 X 4s, 2 X 6s, 2 X 8s etc. It's the same with one inch (actually 3/4") lumber. 5/4" (actually 1") isn't so common as the 1" and 2" lumber, but can be found. Take whatever is available and run it through the table saw to make the widths below. It isn't necessary to have all these sizes before beginning, but the more wood choices, the more variable the projects. Here are the sizes to cut:

> 3/16" thick by 3/4" wide - cut from 1" material
> 3/16" thick by 1" wide - cut from 5/4" material
> 1/4" thick by 1 1/2" wide - cut from 2" material
>
> 1/2" thick by 1" wide - cut from 5/4"
> 1/2" thick by 1 1/2" wide - cut from 2"
>
> 3/4" thick by 3/4" wide - cut from 1"
> 3/4" thick by 1 1/2" wide - cut from 2"
> 3/4" thick by 2" (called 1 X 2) - standard or recut from wider material
> 3/4" thick by 3" (1 X 3) - standard or recut
> 3/4" thick by 4" (1 X 4) - standard or recut

The Wood Choosing Lesson

At first younger children hardly notice the size or shape of a piece of wood. A child might need a 1 X 4 ten inches long for a boat, but return from the wood box with a piece 1/4" thick and 1 1/2" wide.

For younger kids I'll take a model of the project to the wood box and pick up a piece of wood that is obviously much smaller and, holding it right next to the model, say "Hmm... this looks a

Figure 42.
Tracing the pattern.

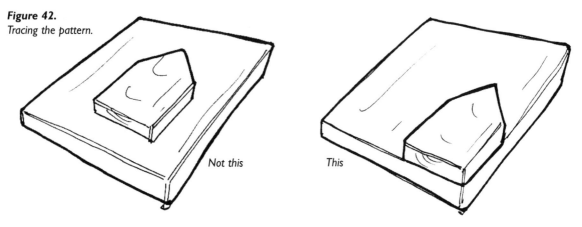

Not this   This

little small." Then I'll compare a larger piece and say, "Too big." The third piece I choose is about right. Most children get the idea before you're halfway through the lesson. Other variations might be something like, "Would this piece work with a saw cut here?" or "This would work but maybe we could find a piece without a big knot." or "These two pieces could both work: which do you like best?"

When the project is traced or drawn on the chosen wood, kids often make the same mistake they make with paper: placing an object they want to copy in the center of the paper. Boats are a classic example. A child will place a boat pattern which is 4" wide in the center of a board 8" wide and draw around it. I'll show how to save two cuts (not to mention wood) by placing the stern corner of the boat on the corner of the wood *(Figure 42)*.

MEASURING AND MARKING

I try to get kids to measure or draw just about everything before they begin cutting. It helps make clear exactly what is to be done before attempting to do it. Not surprisingly, children don't intuitively understand this. They want to start cutting right away. Marking a boat with a straight line makes it easier to cut straight. Drawing helps a child to see what a project might look like before he starts cutting.

Sometimes accurate measuring is important; sometimes it isn't. Pencil holders, for example, could be 11/2" or 4" tall or anywhere in between. A box might be 4" inches square or 6". The base for the flipper can be 10" or 14". The marble roll could be 16" square or 20". These examples require measuring only in a general sense and kids can use a tape measure, can take the measurement from a model, or, as we say in the trade, eyeball it.

When accuracy is more important, a good means of measuring is comparing against a model or pattern. With model boats, for example, I'll make an extra boat to be used as a pattern and label it "pattern." Kids trace around it onto larger pieces. Often the exact piece is not available so the choice becomes: choose a larger piece and cut it down or think about whether the project can be altered to fit the wood available. Sometimes proportion is more important than accuracy.

Sometimes exact (perhaps I should say semi-exact) measurements are important. The legs of a table or opposite sides of a box come to mind. The easiest and most accurate method is to cut one piece and use it as a pattern for the opposite leg or side. Box sides usually come from long precut strips so I demonstrate how to cut the first piece and place it on top of the long strip, making sure the end edges are even, and mark the second piece. To cut four equal sides for a box, the procedure is: cut the first piece and use it as a pattern to measure the second piece. Cut the second piece. Use the first piece (not the second) again to measure the third piece. Mark and cut. It's the same with the last piece.

Kids sometimes mark the pattern length on the precut strip four times before cutting. Nice try, but it won't work. Because each pencil mark and each saw cut will be a little off, inaccuracies compound, resulting in four different length boards. Measuring with a tape at 4", 8", 12" and 16" and then going back and cutting won't work either for the same reason. Repeat cuts the same length (without measuring every time) can be made using the miter block and a stop as explained on page 188.

CHAPTER FOUR · NAILS & SCREWS

NAILS

How to Pound a Nail

Set up a separate pounding area. The best place for nailing is not the workbench (except for the small stuff) but on the floor in an out-of-the-way corner. Nailing at the workbench is distracting for other children, can result in flying nails or pieces of wood, and puts the child too high to swing the hammer effectively.

There is an old saying among woodworkers, "Woodworking is easy. It's getting ready to do the woodworking that's difficult." This is true of nailing. The actual pounding isn't that difficult. The hard part is putting the nail in the right place, getting it started straight, and holding everything together as you are whacking it with a hammer. Here are four steps to help ease children into the art of driving nails.

First Lesson for Very Young Children: Making a Sign

This project consists of a small board with the child's name (or Mom or Dad) outlined in indentations made by three or four taps on a nail. It allows young children to hold a hammer and a nail in position and practice the pounding motion.

Tools
- One nail about three inches long with a big head.
- Small hammer.
- Optional drill.

Materials
- Small board about 3" X 6".
- Sandpaper.
- 1/4" dowel or pencil.
- Optional small piece of string to hang the sign.

Construction

Print the child's name on the board or have her do it herself. The child's job is to tap the nail three or four times every 1/4" inch or so, following the letters. Use the dowel or pencil for a spacer to measure the distance from one hole to the next. The result is the child's name outlined in dots. Then drill two holes in the top of the sign so it can be hung up by the string.

Second Lesson: Nailing into a Firewood Round

For this lesson you'll need:
- Hammer.
- A firewood round. The bigger the better, but even 6" in diameter and 6" high will work. Make sure it sits flat on the floor and doesn't wobble every time it's hit.
- Use 1" roofing nails (big head) for the first lesson. Go to 1¹/₄" or 1¹/₂" nails as competence increases.

    Putting a nail in can be divided into two steps: starting it and driving it in. Begin with 1" roofing nails because the large heads are easier to hit. Hold the nail with one hand and tap it (gently but not too gently) until it will stand by itself *(Figure 43)*. After the nail is standing solidly, it needs to be hit harder. First, move the hand holding the nail at least 6" away from the nail. This may seem obvious, but because beginners focus on the nail and hammer, they often forget. This is why thumbs get mashed. After the extra hand is out of the way, hit the nail hard to drive it in. The hammer should hit the nail head straight on. If it doesn't, the nail will bend off to the side. If the nail bends, it must be straightened before pounding continues. The problem is to bring as much force as possible straight down onto the top of the nail. I tell kids, "Lift the hammer up 8 or 10 inches and then sort of drop it but control and guide it." It's first about guiding the drop and later about assisting the drop *(Figure 44)*.

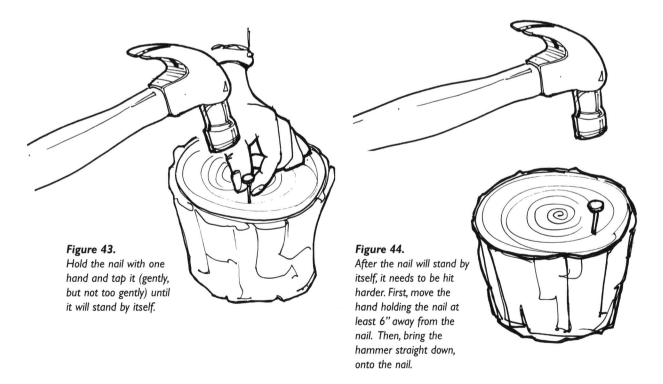

Figure 43.
Hold the nail with one hand and tap it (gently, but not too gently) until it will stand by itself.

Figure 44.
After the nail will stand by itself, it needs to be hit harder. First, move the hand holding the nail at least 6" away from the nail. Then, bring the hammer straight down, onto the nail.

If a child has difficulty, start fifteen or twenty nails so they can drive them in without worrying about getting them started or bending them. After a child can put these in, move on to a longer nail with a smaller head. Older kids like to pound nails into the stump too *(Figure 45)*. It's good practice, and not uncommon for a student to pound 50 or 100 nails. One child at a time at the pounding block is a good idea. If a second child is watching, be sure he has eye protection.

Figure 45.
Pounding nails into a stump is great practice.

Third lesson: Where Nail Placement isn't Critical

After a child has some practice pounding nails into the stump, move her on to a project where placement isn't too critical. The camp stool project (page 114) is a good example. In this project, a piece of plywood is nailed on the bottom of a 2" thick (by 6" or 8" diameter) section of tree trunk. The nails should be uniformly spaced. This also provides an opportunity to introduce a trick that makes fastening two boards together easier: *pound the nails through the first board until they just stick out before even picking up the second board.* Starting the nail, pounding it in, and holding the two boards in position are too many things at once. Here is how to do it:

Referring to the camp stool project again, the plywood piece is placed solidly on the floor (not on the round tree section) and five or six nails are put in so they are just barely poking through the plywood. Then the plywood is placed on the section of tree and the pounding is finished. This trick will also help in a situation where more precision is required, like nailing the edges of a box together or fastening a cabin to a boat, but pilot holes are even better and, in the long run, easier.

Fourth Lesson: Nailing Boards Together Using Pilot Holes

First, a few words about pilot holes. If you try to put a screw into oak (or other hardwood), most likely it will break. Try to put a nail into hardwood and it will bend. Hardwoods, therefore, require a hole for the screw or nail to follow. These holes are called pilot holes and need to be smaller than the nail or screw. For hardwoods, there should be a pilot hole in both the board you are fastening through, and the board you're fastening into.

With softwood, large screws require pilot holes but smaller sheetrock screws can often be put in without them. Nails don't need pilot holes in softwood except near the end of a board to prevent splitting. If a screw breaks, a nails bends, or wood splits as the fastener goes in, pilot holes should have been used. For fancy work, use pilot holes; for utilitarian jobs, try to get by without.

After a child can drive a nail into the stump and nail the plywood to the bottom of the camping stool (or equivalent), the next step is to fasten corners together. This can be discouraging. Boards bounce around, nails go in crooked, and wood splits. To make this operation less frustrating and more successful, have kids lay out and drill pilot holes (through the first board only) which help the fastener go in straight and in the right place.

Here's how to do it:

1. *Fasten through the thin wood into the thick wood (Figure 46a).* For beginners, the wood being nailed into should be at least $3/4$". Anything thinner is hard to hit.

2. *Choose the right length nail,* approximately twice as long as the thickness of the wood the nail first goes through *(Figure 46b).* Left to their own devices, it's common to see

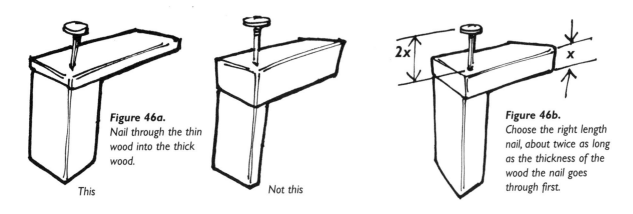

Figure 46a.
Nail through the thin wood into the thick wood.

This

Not this

Figure 46b.
Choose the right length nail, about twice as long as the thickness of the wood the nail goes through first.

children try to pound a 3" nail through a $1/2$" board. Too large a nail will split wood and a small nail won't hold. Demonstrate by pounding a big nail into a small piece of wood so children can watch the wood split, and by fastening two boards together with a small nail and pulling them apart.

3. *Draw a line showing where the two boards meet.* With one board flat on the workbench and the other held on top of it, I say, "Hold the boards even on the outside and mark

the inside" *(Figure 46c)*. I'll demonstrate by holding two boards together while the child marks the inside line.

4. *Mark pilot hole* position halfway between the edge of the board and the line *(Figure 46d)*.

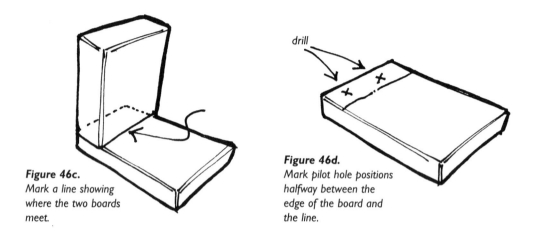

drill

Figure 46c.
Mark a line showing where the two boards meet.

Figure 46d.
Mark pilot hole positions halfway between the edge of the board and the line.

5. *Drill pilot holes.* But first choose the right bit. The pilot hole should be a hair smaller than the nail it is piloting *(Figure 46e)*.

6. *Tap the nails* into the first board till they just barely stick out *(Figure 46f)*.

7. *Position the boards and nail.* The nail points should stick into the second board and keep the two pieces in position. Have the child pound the first nail while you hold the boards together *(Figure 46g)*.

8. *Countersink.* Any nails sticking out on the bottom of a project should be set below the surface of the wood with a nail set. See countersinking, page 46.

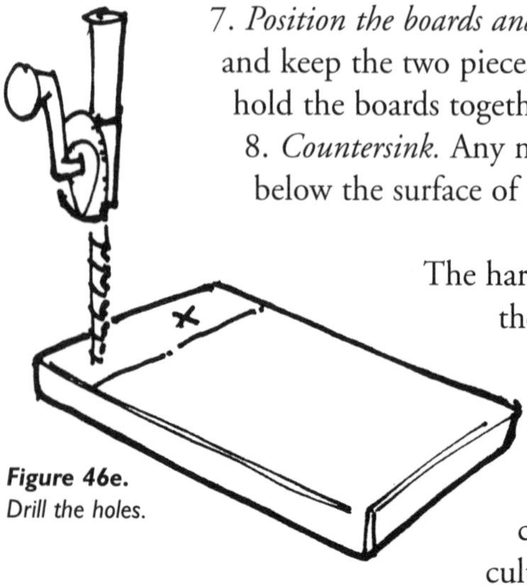

Figure 46e.
Drill the holes.

The hardest part of nailing is not swinging the hammer but holding the boards solidly in position. The bottom board, the one the nail is going into, must be firmly backed up against the floor or a solid block. If it is not, the energy from the hammer goes into bouncing the wood around, rather than into the nail. This is the reason pounding nails on carpet, on a light duty workbench, or in a vice is more difficult than pounding nails into wood backed up by the solid floor or a pounding block.

At first I try to convince kids to drill pilot holes for every nail. Later, after competence develops, pilot holes may be omitted but it's still a good idea to mark the nail positions before pounding them. It is possible for kids to drive nails without pilot holes and if someone wants to try, that's fine with me. I just tell him that I don't want any nails left sticking out, because someone could get poked. Usually there will be a few sticking out and I'll demonstrate how to pound those back through with a nail set and pull them out with a hammer.

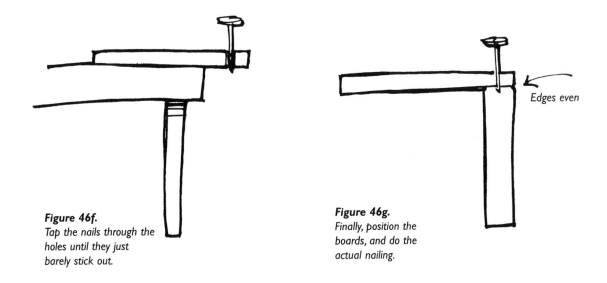

Figure 46f.
Tap the nails through the holes until they just barely stick out.

Figure 46g.
Finally, position the boards, and do the actual nailing.

Edges even

SCREWS

Materials

- Sheetrock screws of various lengths: $7/8$", $1^1/4$", and $1^5/8$" cover most situations.
- A drill bit the size the screw would be if it didn't have any threads, for drilling a pilot hole for the screw to follow.
- A countersink (see page 46) to widen the top of the pilot hole so the screw head will sink below the surface of the board. This is especially important on the bottom of a project that might end up on the dining room table.

Pilot Holes & Countersinking

Laying out and drilling a pilot hole for a screw is similar to the procedure for a nail. Widen the pilot hole by inserting the cutting end of the countersink into the pilot hole and rotating a few times until the hole is deep enough to receive the screw head. If a countersink is not available, a $1/2$" drill bit will work.

After the hole is drilled and countersunk, choose the right length screw (twice the thickness of the board the screw is going through), and start the screw in the pilot hole. Put it all the way through the board until it just barely pokes through the other side. If there is more than one screw, start them all.

Put the second board (the one you are fastening into) in the vice. Have a helper hold the board with the screws in position and sink the screws the rest of the way. Once the screw starts biting into the second board it becomes more difficult to turn. Switch to a brace with a screwdriver bit. A brace is easier to turn but will take a little help and practice, especially for younger children. Be careful not to tighten the screw too much or the threads holding the screw may strip out.

Shop Setup

Screws are handy for shop setup. All my vices are fastened to the workbench with screws. So are the miter block and drill press. Screws make good temporary fastenings because they come out easily, enabling a vice or a miter box to be repositioned quickly. I put most of the shop setup screws in with a brace.

Safety Alert

Even though I try to avoid it, sometimes screws end up near the pounding block and children will try to pound them in with a hammer. This is not a good idea. Screws are designed to twist in and consequently require incredible amounts of force to drive with a hammer. Screws are also made from a harder steel so they tend to break rather than bend like a nail. This combination of more force and harder steel can result in broken screws zinging around the room. Try to keep screws separate from nails and away from the pounding block.

Choosing Nails or Screws

Screws make a stronger joint, but often nails are strong enough. Nails are easier to drive than screws, which is the attraction, but if they go in crooked or miss their target, any speed advantage is lost. If glue is added to a nail joint (and you can wait for it to dry), the difference in strength between nail and screw is negligible. The step stool, (page 146) goes together with screws; I didn't want it coming apart with someone standing on it. Nails alone might work loose. If the joints are tight and fit well (probably not the case with kids), glue and nails would work, too. For the camping stool I have kids use nails (and glue) to fasten the plywood circle to the bottom of the seat. Nails are good in this case because it doesn't matter exactly where they go or even if they are perfectly straight. I have kids nail bigger boxes together because nails are strong enough and a bit easier; screws would be stronger, however.

CHAPTER FIVE · PROJECTS

Projects are the bait to lure kids into practicing sawing, nailing, and drilling and developing the skills of planning, organizing, and persisting. The more interesting, clever, or beautiful a project, the more motivated a child will be to build it.

Even when projects are "easy," it often takes more than one try to work out successful construction details. Tops are a good example. First, I tried having kids cut the round disk for the top body on their own, using the hand-operated drill press. This had worked at home with my own kids but with ten kids and one drill press there was a bottleneck at the drill press. Next, I tried round branches for the top body. For older kids, this worked about half the time, not a great success rate. Younger children had trouble making an even cut and drilling a straight center hole so success was even more elusive. Finally, I precut the round top disk at home with the drill press. This worked much better and everyone was able to build a successful top. It still took me a class or two to figure out a way for kids to sharpen the center shaft (hand pencil sharpener) and tap it in. With all the details worked out, tops became my introductory project for preschoolers. The only problem was, now tops were too easy for the older kids. Eventually, I discovered a tool called a "center finder" which allowed older kids to make successful tops from tree branches.

Models

Models help kids visualize possibilities. It's ten times more effective to show a child a model of a boat (or whatever) and ask, "Would you like to build one of these?" than it is to ask, "Would you like to build a boat?" Children respond to the item, not the words.

The best models are built by kids. Many of mine were built by my own children or were given to me by children from my classes. Sometimes I'll build a project myself, but I'm careful to keep it simple.

One summer I had the idea for a log cabin project. I cut up strips of wood for the logs and built a little house which I didn't really like, but put out anyway to see if anyone was interested. For a long time the kids hardly looked at it. Then one day I asked, "Would you like to make log cabins tomorrow?" Most kids wanted to try, and at the end of "log cabin" day we had a rather awesome display of interesting and clever mini log cabins. Mine was by far the most boring, but as a model it served its purpose.

First Projects

Often the first projects young children make are little pieces of wood assembled (or not) in some seemingly haphazard form. I remember a $3^1/2$-year-old boy who was so ecstatically happy at learning to use the saw he spent the whole afternoon cutting little pieces of wood which he very carefully kept track of and took home. His project required imagination, tool use, organization, and planning. Shop became his favorite subject.

How I Present a Project

In one sense the presentation of a project is the same regardless of age. Older children will naturally absorb more steps faster, but they still have to go through the same steps.

I'll start by saying something like, "You've all done puzzles before, haven't you? Then you know that to do a puzzle, the right pieces must go in the right place or you won't finish the puzzle. It is the same with building. The right pieces in the right place."

"Today we're going to make a box (or whatever). Here is the finished box. First we'll make the sides, four pieces the same length." For older kids I'll add some choice by saying and demonstrating, "If you want a rectangular box, opposite sides of the box have to be the same size. Here is how to make the sides come out the same length."

Often I'll wait after this step until everyone is ready for the next step. "The next step is to put the sides together. Here is how to do it. Here is how to measure the pieces for the bottom." And so on, step-by-step. After a few projects, as children gain confidence, I start turning over some of the planning to the kids by asking something like, "How should we start this project?" or by saying, "I forget what to do next. Can you help me out?"

Choosing Projects

The following projects are divided, roughly, in order of complexity. Choose projects appropriate for the child's skill level. Older children often like to build the easier projects, but younger children should hone their skills before attempting the more complicated projects.

The idea is to start with the easier projects and build skills. Children will get more pleasure (not to mention learn more) from building a pencil holder themselves than from helping an adult construct a more complicated project. A little frustration is OK, but prolonged frustration or lots of adult help means a project is too complicated.

If you build the same projects over and over they will evolve as you naturally think of improvements and changes. The directions given are meant more as a take-off point than as the only way to construct a project. If you think of an alternate way to do something, by all means try it.

WOOD SANDING

Most kids will be amazed how sanding and a little oil can turn a grubby piece of wood into a thing of beauty. They will want to try it. Competence will vary. There are what I call the Q & D (quick and dirty) sanders who are in a hurry. I make sure they get the slivers off, and encourage them (usually to no avail) to slow down. For the gung-ho sanders I'll bring out the 220 grit paper. Many children will try and make their wood as smooth as glass. Quite a few kids will make a wood collection and start thinking about a box to put it in. *Figure 47* shows a branch just after it was cut (left), and the same branch after it's been sanded (right).

Tools
- Eye protection.
- Saw and vice if kids are cutting their own pieces.
- Sandpaper 80 and 220 grit.

Materials
Small pieces (approximately 3/4" X 3/4" X 3/4") of scrap wood: different kinds, different shapes, and round sections from branches are good. Or, have small branches and boards available so kids can cut small pieces themselves.

Sanding Lesson
I'll choose a piece of wood. With younger children, I'll start with a round part of a branch because it has only two sides to sand. I'll sand it myself, pressing down hard to get results quickly, stopping a couple of times to show how the scratches disappear and letting them feel the smoothness. I save this piece for the oiling lesson. Then it is the child's turn to choose or cut a piece of wood and sand it. Kids keep and take home their wood or they can make a key chain or wood collection.

Figure 47.
The wood on the left has been cut, but not sanded. The wood on the right has been sanded.

OILING WOOD

After a good sanding job, oiling can transform many woods from ho-hum to beautiful. Kids appreciate this and want to do it *(Figure 48)*. The tendency is to use too much oil, which doesn't hurt anything but can make a mess. For preschoolers, I confine this activity to small pieces of wood and keep the paint brushes small. Be sure to oil after gluing because glue will not stick to an oiled surface.

Materials
- Mineral oil.
- Cotton swabs, small paint brush, or eye dropper.
- Paper towels.

Oiling Lesson

Lay out a paper towel. Place the sanded wood in the center. Dab a few drops of oil on the wood and spread with a cotton swab, brush, or finger. Dry with a paper towel and put on the shelf for a few minutes to dry. *Figure 49* shows Billy and Parker oiling their boxes.

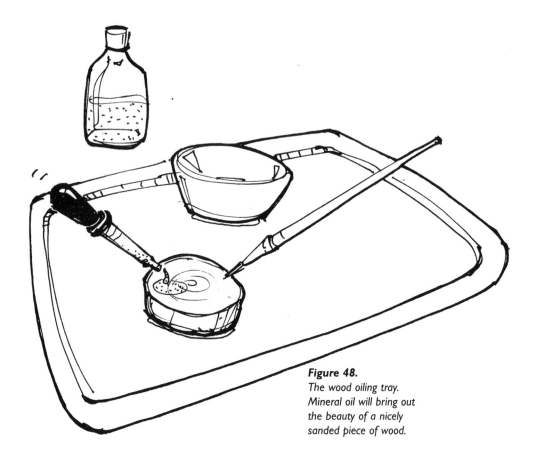

Figure 48.
The wood oiling tray. Mineral oil will bring out the beauty of a nicely sanded piece of wood.

Figure 49.
Billy and Parker intent on oiling their boxes.

TOPS I: Precut Disks

I have two ways of making tops *(Figure 50)*. The first method, using precut disks, involves more preparation but is easier for kids to build. It is a good first project when preschoolers have their heads full of new tools and safety information. The second method (see Tops II) is more complicated. It's for older kids who have built a few projects and can pay a bit more attention to the details.

Figure 50.
Tops made with precut disks.

Adult Preparation

A parent, teacher, or volunteer needs to cut the top disks.

Tools

- A brace or a drill press.
- A 1¹/₂" hole saw *(Figure 51)*. A hole saw costs between ten and fifteen dollars (2005 prices). If you buy a hole saw to make just a few tops, each top gets expensive. Maybe you can find someone who would lend you a hole saw. Be sure to return it right away. Woodworkers get irritated when their tools aren't returned.
- Eye protection.

Figure 51.
A hole saw and two top disks.

Materials

- 1/4" plywood. Thicker wood will work but is more work, especially if you are cutting the disks by hand.

Cutting the Disks

There are two ways to do this: by hand with a brace, or with a drill press. If you need just a few disks, do it by hand. A few fourth or fifth graders can handle a brace with a hole saw, but mostly it's for adults. The hard part is not just cutting the disks, but getting them out of the hole saw. To do this, drill almost all the way through from one side, flip the board over, and finish the hole from the other side. This leaves only a little of the disk inside the hole saw and it can usually be twisted out by hand. If the disk inadvertently ends up inside the hole saw, pry it out with screwdrivers. **Be careful of the sharp teeth on the hole saw.**

If you want to make lots of tops, find someone with a drill press to cut the disks quickly. Ask a neighborhood woodworker, a shop teacher, or someone at the senior volunteer center. Many woodworkers will be glad to help.

Kids: Making Tops

Tools

- Small hand pencil sharpener.
- Vice.
- Sandpaper glued to boards and fastened to the workbench.
- Small piece of 1/2" plywood with a 1/2" hole. Woodworkers would call this a jig which is just a device to make construction easier.
- A keyhole saw with hacksaw blade.
- Eye protection.

Materials

- 1/4" dowel 3" long for each top.
- Top disks (see preparation above).
- Paint or markers.

Construction

1. Sand the disk.
2. Cut the center dowel about 3" long.
3. Sharpen dowel to a dull point with a hand pencil sharpener.

4. Place the disk on top of the jig with the hole in the disk over the hole in the jig *(Figure 52)*. Tap the dowel through the hole of the disk and down through the hole in the jig until it hits the workbench. The jig makes it so the dowel comes out on the bottom of the top just the right amount.

5. Test to be sure it works.

6. Decorate with oil, paint, or markers. One student discovered that alternating blue and yellow stripes painted on his top turned to green when he spun the top. This set off a frenzy of color mixing to see what colors could be produced.

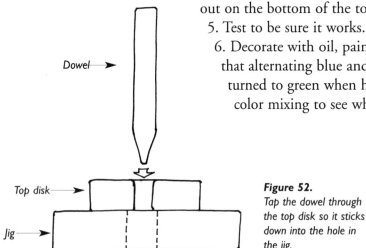

Figure 52.
Tap the dowel through the top disk so it sticks down into the hole in the jig.

Troubleshooting

Sometimes a finished top will wobble a bit or even so much that it won't stand up. This is because it is out of balance, usually because the hole is off-center, but it could also be an uneven disk. Place the defective top on the jaws of a slightly opened vice with each side of the disk supported on opposite sides of the vice and the dowel protruding down between the vice jaws. Tap the dowel out (down between vice jaws) and then try another disk.

You can demonstrate the idea of "out of balance" by putting a small piece of clay on a good top and spinning it. Or try to fix an out of balance top by adding a dollop of clay to the outer rim.

TOPS II: Do-It-Yourself Disks

Older kids like to make tops too, but it's too easy if the disks are already cut. They can try the brace with the hole saw and cut their own disks or they can try the following design using branches (*Figure 53*).

Tools

- Keyhole saw with a hacksaw blade.
- Sandpaper.
- Vice.
- Drill with a bit to match the dowel.
- A center finder, available at good hardware stores for about $3.50.

- Handsaw.
- Eye protection.
- Surform plane.

Figure 53.
A top made from a branch of a locust tree.

Materials

- About 3" of ¹/4" dowel
- Mineral oil, markers, and paint.
- A bit of clay for adjusting top balance.
- Tree branches between 1¹/2" and 2¹/2" in diameter as close to round as possible.

Construction

Beautiful tops can be made from a section of tree branch, but are they balanced enough to spin? Variables influencing balance are: how round is the tree branch? how uniform is the slice thickness? and how close is the hole to center?

1. Start by choosing a branch as close to round as possible. Cut a slice of uniform thickness. Small variations are OK but a wedge-shaped section won't work.
2. Drill a hole in the center of the branch. How to find the center? With a little practice, eyeballing will work, but a center finder *(Figure 54)* is more accurate. A center finder is an easy-to-use guide (perfect for kids) for drawing straight lines across a circle. It comes with directions. Two straight lines drawn across a circle at approximately 90 degrees from each other will cross in the center. Since the branch won't be perfectly round, the hole won't be in the exact center, but it's often close enough. Drill the hole as straight as possible.

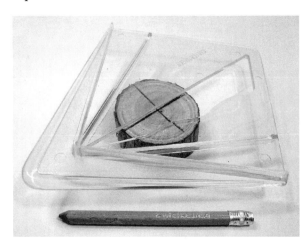

Figure 54.
A center finder provides a guide for drawing two lines (offset 90 degrees) across a circle. The center of the circle is located where the lines cross.

3. Cut the center dowel and sharpen it the same as for the first top.
4. Sand.
5. Place the disk on top of the jig with the hole in the disk over the hole in the jig. Tap the dowel through the hole of the disk down through the hole in the jig until it hits the workbench. The jig makes it so the dowel comes out on the bottom of the top just the right amount. Test the top to make sure it spins.
6. Oil and/or decorate with paint or markers.

Troubleshooting

A top made from a branch will usually wobble a bit because there are too many variables to get exactly right for it to spin perfectly. If the top doesn't spin at all, don't give up yet. Examine the disk again. Is the branch as round as you thought it was? If it isn't, (maybe it's oval shaped) try cutting or sanding away parts to make the disk closer to round.

Looking down on the top of the top, does the dowel appear close to the center? If it's just a little off, try removing wood to make the circle rounder. Is the branch thicker on one edge than the other? If it is, removing wood from the heavy side (with sandpaper or Surform) might help. Occasionally, there is too much to be done and it's easier to start over from the beginning, trying to be a little more careful. I continue to learn this lesson.

KEY CHAIN

Making a key chain combines sanding and oiling with sawing and drilling. Tying the knot to attach the key to the key fob can also be a lesson *(Figure 55)*.

Tools

- Saw.
- Vice.
- Sandpaper, 80 and 220 grit glued to boards fastened to the workbench.
- Eye protection.
- Hand drill or spiral screwdriver and $1/8$" drill bit.

Materials

- Paper towels.
- Small dry tree branches, $3/4$"-1" in diameter: maple, cedar, birch, oak.
- Heavy string or thin strip of leather to tie keys to fob.
- Mineral oil in a small shallow dish and a tiny paint brush or cotton swab.
- Blank keys. Any place that makes keys will have a box of mistakes they can usually be talked out of.

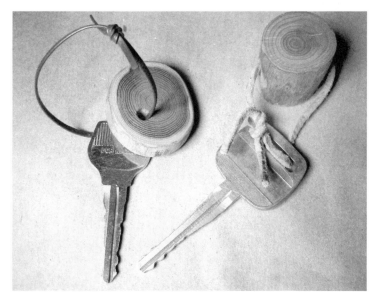

Figure 55.
Two key chains. The wood on the left is locust; on the right is red cedar.

Construction

1. Choose and cut wood.
2. Sand the ends of the wood smooth.
3. Drill hole in the wood.
4. Oil the wood.
5. Tie key on with a square knot.

WOOD MATCHING

The first year I taught woodworking, I had some small pieces of wood for my young carpenters to sand. A youngster asked, "You mean each tree has a different-looking wood?" As it happened, there was a pile of wood next to the shop where we were working. I suggested he could see for himself by searching through this woodpile. Over the next few days several students spent hours cutting, sanding, and oiling pieces from the woodpile. This experience gave me the idea to make a simple matching game with different kinds of wood.

I sanded and oiled two pieces each of several kinds of wood. I glued one of the matching pieces to a card. On the card I wrote the name of the wood. Children lay out the cards and then match the loose pieces of wood to their "twins" on the card. Fir to fir. Oak to oak, etc. *Figure 56* shows the wood matching project.

A few kids liked this game so much they wanted to make a set to take home. This project is just a combination of wood sanding and wood oiling.

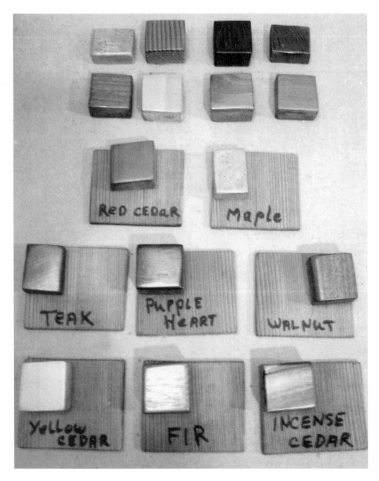

Figure 56.
Wood matching. A simple game created when a child asked, "you mean each tree has a different looking wood?"

Tools

- Vice.
- Handsaw.
- Low-temperature hot glue gun and glue sticks. White glue works well too, but takes longer to dry.
- Eye protection.
- Sandpaper, 80 grit and 220 grit.

Materials

- Mineral oil.
- Stiff paper. I use card stock. Get enough to make cards for each type of wood sanded.
- Small pieces of different kinds of wood. I choose fir, red cedar, yellow cedar, incense cedar, oak, pine, teak, mahogany and maple but any wood that sands up to look nice is good. Local woods are good. Any woodworker or cabinet shop should be able help you locate different samples.

Construction

1. Cut two similar pieces of each kind of wood.
2. Sand each piece of wood to a fine finish.
3. Glue one piece of each type of wood to the top of a 4" X 5" piece of card stock paper and write the type of wood at the bottom of the card. Younger kids will need help with the writing.
4. Put the separate matching pieces of wood in a basket or small box. Kids over five years old can make the box (page 119) themselves.

PUZZLES I: Using Precut Puzzle Blanks

For younger kids who would have difficulty using a coping saw, I make what I call puzzle blanks *(Figure 57)*. These blanks are just a plywood square with the center section cut out in one piece. The kids' job is to draw a picture on this center section, and then cut it into pieces with a handsaw, thus creating the puzzle. I did this project often with four-year-olds at a Montessori school. Older kids like to make puzzles too, but I have them make their own blanks using a coping saw. It's a good coping saw project for beginners because it's not necessary to precisely follow a line when cutting.

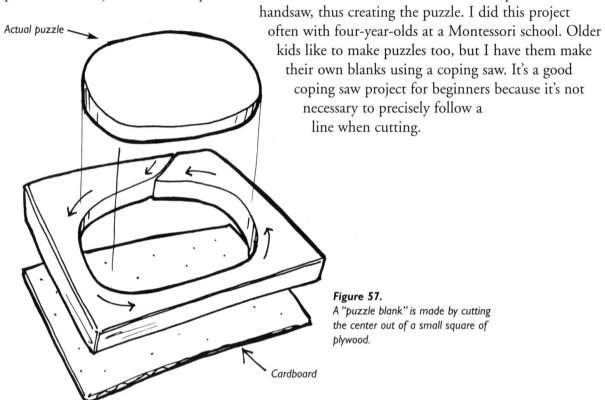

Actual puzzle

Figure 57.
A "puzzle blank" is made by cutting the center out of a small square of plywood.

Cardboard

Adult Preparation

A parent, teacher, or volunteer needs to make the puzzle blanks for younger kids.

Tools
- Mat knife or a sharp knife.
- Eye protection.
- A vice is nice if you are going to cut the blanks by hand.
- Coping saw, band saw, a tabletop jigsaw, or saber saw.

Materials
- A small piece of cardboard to cover the back of each puzzle.
- 6" X 6" squares of 1/4" pressboard (like particle board, only without the glue) or plywood with a smooth finish.

Construction

1. If you only need a few blanks, cut them with a coping saw. If you need a stack of blanks you'll need help from a volunteer woodworker with a band saw, tabletop jigsaw, or a hand-held saber saw. First cut out 6" X 6" (approximately) squares.
2. Once the squares are cut out, go back and cut out the center of each square *(Figure 57)*. This will be the actual puzzle—the piece the kids will cut into pieces.
3. Finally cut a piece of cardboard to fit the bottom of each puzzle blank. You can use a mat knife or scissors to cut the cardboard.
   Safety Note: Mat knives are dangerous. Every carpenter I know has sliced him/herself at least once using a mat knife. Don't let kids use them.

Kids: Making the Puzzle

Tools

- Handsaw.
- Vice.
- Low-temp hot glue gun and glue sticks.
- Markers.
- Eye protection.

Materials

- 6" X 6" piece of $1/4$" pressboard (or plywood) with a smooth surface for each project.
- 6" X 6" piece of cardboard for backing each puzzle.

Construction

1. Draw a picture on the puzzle blank with felt pens.
2. Hot glue the outside of the puzzle blank to the cardboard. Four drops of glue, one in each corner, is usually enough.
3. Cut the picture into pieces to make the puzzle. The first time I tried this project, several kids cut their picture into so many tiny pieces they were unable to put them back together. Now I suggest cutting the puzzle into two pieces and then cutting each of those pieces into two more pieces. After they've made a four-piece puzzle, they can test it and see if they want to make a few more pieces.

PUZZLES II: Kids Cut Their Own Blanks

Tools

- Handsaw.
- Sandpaper.
- Vice.
- Keyhole saw to cut cardboard in case scissors don't work.
- Low-temperature hot glue gun and glue sticks.
- Coping saw.
- Scissors to cut cardboard.
- Eye protection.

Materials

- Small pieces of 1/4" pressboard or plywood with a smooth finish.
- Cardboard to form the back of the puzzle. Get thin cardboard or heavy paper that can be cut with scissors.
- Markers.

Construction

1. Cut a square (any shape really) for the puzzle from pressboard or plywood.
2. Draw a circle in the center of this square (the actual puzzle) and cut it out with a coping saw (*Figure 57,* page 78).
3. Hot glue cardboard to the back of the piece that frames the puzzle. Four drops of glue, one in each corner, is usually enough.
4. Draw a picture on the center circle with markers and then cut it into pieces, but not too many. *Figure 58* shows four kid-constructed puzzles.

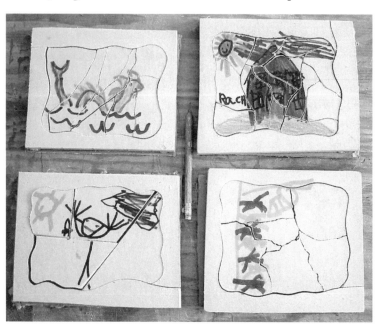

Figure 58.
Four puzzles constructed by kids.

MAKING LOST PUZZLE PIECES

One day I noticed a teacher taking an arm load of puzzles from storage and I asked if she was taking new puzzles to school. No, she was throwing them away because of missing pieces. It galled me that, in this era of tight budgets for children, literally hundreds of dollars of good puzzles were going to be thrown away because of missing pieces. I took them home and, in a few minutes, made pieces for most of them. It's not rocket science. Do it yourself once or twice and then teach the kids to do it! I taught kindergartners to do it, but I had to help with the coping saw.

Tools

- Vice.
- Sandpaper.
- Keyhole saw might work best if pieces are small.
- Coping saw.
- Eye protection.

Materials

- Pencil and paper.
- Paint to match puzzle piece.
- Clear tape.
- A small piece of plywood the same thickness as missing puzzle piece. I use plywood because thin pieces don't split when cut, and because it is easier to find in the thicknesses needed. Nearly any carpenter will have miscellaneous small pieces of wood. If you obtain several pieces of standard thicknesses ($1/8"$, $3/16"$, $1/4"$, $3/8"$, $1/2"$), you will have enough to wood to replace puzzle pieces for decades.

Figure 59.
A lost puzzle piece pattern can be made by placing paper in the missing space and drawing the puzzle shape on it (upper left), or by taping paper over the top of the missing piece and outlining the edge of the hole with a pencil (lower right).

Construction

1. Make a pattern of the lost piece. One method is to tape a piece of paper over the hole left by the missing piece. Then lightly draw back and forth, using the flat side of a pencil, around the hole. The shape of the missing piece will be outlined by a dark pencil line. Cut this pattern out.

   Another method is to take the puzzle apart (just around the missing piece) and place a piece of paper on the bottom of the puzzle. Then put the puzzle back together and draw the shape of the missing piece onto the paper. Cut this paper piece out. *Figure 59* shows both methods of making patterns.

2. Find wood the same thickness as the lost piece and trace around the paper pattern onto the wood.

3. Put the wood with the pattern traced on it in a vice and cut it out with a coping saw. If you haven't used a coping saw, read about coping saws (page 29) in the tool section. After the puzzle piece is cut out, see if it will fit into the puzzle. If it doesn't fit, use sand paper or saw to make adjustments.

4. After the piece fits, paint it to match the rest of the puzzle.

SCULPTURE

Although sculpture is an easy project, children will absorb many basic construction techniques. They begin to learn:

- How long to hold the glue before it dries.
- How much glue is necessary.
- How to keep from getting burned by the glue.
- How to strengthen a joint by bracing it.
- That some ways of putting things together don't work.
- That heavy pieces need to go on the bottom.
- That there are usually several ways to approach a construction problem.
- That glue won't hold larger things together.

I love the way sculpture is self-correcting. The teacher's role is minimal. I confine my help to something like, "Would a brace here help?" or "What would happen if you did X or Y?" Two child-constructed sculptures are shown below in *Figures 60a and b.*

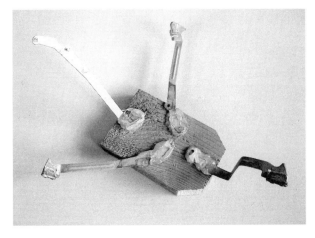

Figure 60a.
This sculpture was made from bent typewriter keys.

Figure 60b.
This figure shows a clever use of cloths pins and yarn.

Tools
- Saw.
- Eye protection.

- Vice.
- Low-temperature hot glue gun and glue sticks.

Materials

- Miscellaneous parts from taking apart VCRs: nuts, bolts, screws, motors, wire, etc. See Take-Apart, page 191.
- Small wood scraps. I keep a box of small pieces cut from other projects for just this purpose. Kids can choose pieces from this box or cut their own.
- 6" X 6" cardboard for base of sculpture. Wood can also be used.
- Film canisters (available anywhere film is processed).

Construction

I don't really give instructions for making sculptures. I have a couple of examples available, preferably constructed by kids, and as many materials as possible. Review glue gun safety. *Figure 61* below shows Parker and the beginnings of a film canister sculpture.

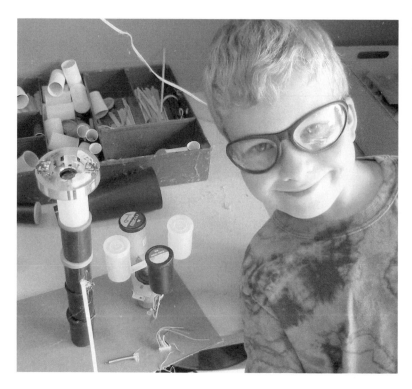

Figure 61.
Parker and the beginnings of his film canister sculpture.

PENCIL HOLDER

Once I was working with 8th graders building a log shelter and the kids were cutting the ends off of the log rafters to even them up. I picked up one of the round cut-off ends (about 3" long and 3" in diameter) and mentioned that I worked with preschoolers and they made pencil holders from similar branches by sanding and drilling holes in them. At the end of the class every kid had asked to take a cut-off piece home so they could make a pencil holder. *Figure 62* shows two pencil holders.

Figure 62.
Two pencil holders made from branches. Pencil holders make great presents.

Tools

- Vice.
- Drill, brace and bit, or drill press.
- Handsaw.
- Eye protection.
- Clamp for holding wood if drill or brace is used on the floor.
- Sandpaper, 80 and 220 grit (see sanding lesson, pages 47-48) glued to boards which in turn are fastened to the workbench.

Materials

Branches about 2 to 4 inches in diameter. Unfortunately, recently cut wood (called green) will contain too much water to use. Saws don't cut green wood easily and, if green-wood is cut into small pieces (such as pencil holders) it will dry out rapidly, causing cracking (which woodworkers call checking). Dry the wood by cutting it into short lengths, painting the ends (to slow the drying), and storing in a cool, dry place for a few months. If branches have been on the ground for a while they might already be dry enough to use, if they aren't checked too badly. Local woods are great. I use cedar, maple, and birch but stay away from fir and pine because of the high sap content.

Construction

1. Kids choose a branch.
2. Measure approximate length against the example.
3. Cut to length and sand the top.
4. Drill holes: several $5/16$" holes, about $3/4$" deep.

FURNITURE

All kinds of small furniture can be made from thin strips of wood and put together with hot glue. Tables, chairs, and beds are favorites *(Figure 63)*. This is a great project for very young children, although one summer two 6th grade girls made an elaborate two-story doll house and furnished it with miniature furniture. Another child expanded this idea to include a miniature playground complete with teeter-totter, swings, and a slide.

Figure 63.
Miniature furniture constructed (mostly) from thin strips of wood.

Adult Preparation

A parent, teacher, or volunteer cuts the strips children will use for the furniture. Cut 2 X 4s and 1 X 4s into thin strips with a table saw. Anyone who has and knows how to use a table saw will be able to whip up a good pile of strips in no time at all.

Kids: Building Furniture

Tools
- Miter block (page 187).
- Sandpaper.
- Eye protection.
- Low-temperature hot glue gun and glue sticks.

- Handsaw.
- Vice.

Materials

- 1¹/₂" X ¹/₄" strips cut from 2" wood.
- ³/₄" X ³/₁₆" strips cut from any 1" thick wood.
- Small pieces of scrap cloth to make tablecloths, blankets, or seat covers.
- Short lengths of 1 X 2 for tabletops.
- Small branch 2-3" in diameter for alternate round tabletop.
- ¹/₄" dowels for table legs.
- Small pieces of ¹/₄" plywood (plywood won't split) for tabletops.

Bench Table

The bench table has two wide legs, running the width of the table *(Figure 64)*.

1. Cut the top first to the desired length from a 1¹/₂" X ¹/₄" strip.
2. Then cut two shorter legs. Use the first leg as a pattern for the second leg so both legs will come out the same length. The miter block (Appendix, page 187) will ensure straight cuts.
3. Sand all pieces.
4. Glue the legs to the underside of the table, back a bit from the end, with hot glue.
5. The tabletop can be oiled to bring out the beauty of the wood, but glue the legs on first as hot glue will not stick to an oiled surface.

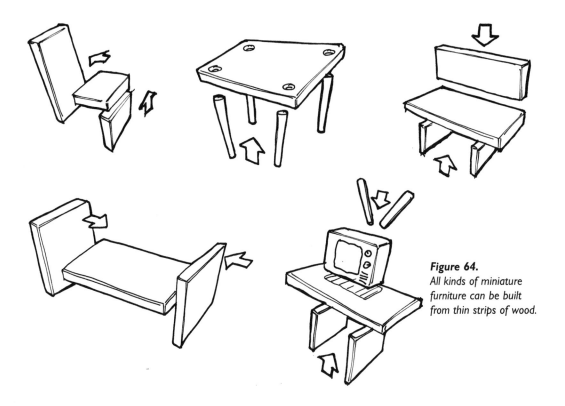

Figure 64.
All kinds of miniature furniture can be built from thin strips of wood.

Table with Round Legs

1. Cut the tabletop. $1/8$" or $1/4$" plywood is a good choice for this project because it won't split when the holes for the legs are drilled. A $3/8$" thick section from a branch 2" or 3" in diameter also makes a good table top, but care must be taken when drilling the holes. Sand.
2. Drill four $1/4$" holes, one near each corner of the tabletop. The holes should be back at least $5/16$" from the edges or the wood may split.
3. Cut four $1/4$" dowels $1^1/2$" long for the legs. Glue these dowels into the holes in the corners of the table. Re-sand the tabletop if the legs stick up a bit.
4. Oil or decorate after legs have been installed.

Chairs

1. Make the pieces first. Use either $3/4$" or $1^1/2$" wide strips. A piece about 2" or $2^1/2$" long forms the back of the chair while two pieces each 1" long form the seat and front leg. Unless the builder can make straight cuts freehand, I encourage using the miter block for all cuts.
2. Sand.
3. Assemble. Glue the two small pieces (leg and seat) together first to form a 90 degree angle. This angle piece can then be glued to the upright chair back and the chair seat will come out level. If the seat is glued to the back first, it must be at the same height as the front leg or the chair seat will be lopsided. Keep models for children to copy. See *Figure 65* to see how one child made furniture from branches.

Figure 65.
A student created this set of small furniture from branches.

AIRPLANES, RAFTS & PEOPLE FROM FILM CANISTERS

Besides being useful as tunnels for the marble roll (page 133) or catchers for the flipper project (page 130), film canisters can be used to make a variety of sculpture-toy projects. People, airplanes, and rafts are popular, but kids will come up with all sorts of ideas and variations themselves.

Tools
- Handsaw.
- Vice.
- Wire cutters for cutting wire and craft sticks.
- Drill and bits for drilling holes for propeller or wheels.
- Eye protection.
- Low-temp hot glue gun and glue sticks.

Materials
- Wire from VCRs for hair or raft rigging.
- Cloth for raft sail.
- Miscellaneous small scraps of wood.
- Markers and paint.
- Film canisters. These are available for the asking just about anywhere photos are processed. Canister lids can be used for wheels.
- Craft or popsicle sticks for propeller, struts, tiller, or rudder.
- Coffee stir sticks for yards (the nautical term for cross members at the top and bottom of a square sail), rails, and wheel spokes.
- 1/4" dowels for raft masts. Larger dowels or broom handles for smokestacks.
- Thin pieces of wood for airplane wings and tail or raft decks. 1/8" strips cut lengthwise from a two-foot 2 X 4 work well.
- Small nuts, bolts, and screws and miscellaneous pieces from taking VCRs apart.
- Scraps of shelf paper make great decorations for airplane wings.
- 1/8" sections cut from 1/2" or 3/4" black automotive hose for boat bumpers (imitation tires). Adults should cut these with a sharp knife.

Construction Tips
1. Wire cutters can be used to cut popsicle sticks. Put the popsicle stick between the wire cutter blades and crimp the stick but don't try to cut all the way through it. As you hold the cutters tightly closed with one hand, wiggle the protruding end of the stick up and down with the other hand. It should break without much difficulty. **Safety Note:** I don't allow the wire cutters to be used on the same table as the glue guns. Kids might accidentally cut through the electrical cords. The only way I have found to reliably keep the cutters away from the glue guns is to tie them to another table. As a double safety precaution, all electrical outlets should have ground fault interrupters to prevent accidental electrical shock.
2. To put a screw into a film canister, (for eyes or to hold a propeller, for example) you

must first drill a hole in the canister. Slide it over a $^3/_4$" dowel (a length of broom handle will work) sticking out of a vice. Start the hole by lightly tapping a nail in the desired spot. Remove the nail and then drill the hole. If you don't demonstrate this method, children will either be squashing the canister in the vice or be chasing it around the workbench with a drill.

Film Canister Airplane

- Three or four canisters glued together, end to end, form the airplane body *(Figure 66)*. The open end of a canister (lid end) should face forward if a propeller is desired. The propeller can then be fastened to the lid as described below.
- Wings, tail, and rudder are made from the thin strips cut from a 2 X 4 or from craft sticks.
- One half of a craft stick can be used as a strut to support each wheel. Wheels can be made from canister lids or from thin sections of dowels. Making the wheels spin, however, gets complicated. See Wheels, page 152.

Figure 66.
An airplane constructed from film canisters, wood scraps, and popsicle sticks.

- To make a propeller that spins, you will need: $^1/_2$ a craft (popsicle) stick, a small screw, a hand drill, and two drill bits: One smaller than the screw, one just larger than the screw. Here is how to put it together:
- Drill a hole in the center of the lid (smaller bit) by putting the lid in the vice vertically and holding the drill horizontally.
- Drill a hole in the center of the craft stick. Use the larger bit so the hole will be bigger than the screw, allowing the propeller to turn freely. Drilling through a thin popsicle stick without splitting it is tricky, so easy does it. Put the screw through the propeller stick and then through the hole in the canister cap. Place a dab of hot glue on the end of the screw so it won't work out as the propeller spins. Place the cap on the front airplane body canister. Decorate with paint or markers.

Film Canister Raft

- Make the raft body *(Figure 67)* by gluing nine (more or less) canisters together. Leaving the lids on will make each canister watertight.
- Make the deck on top of the canisters with craft sticks or thin strips of 2 X 4 hot glued to the canisters.
- Make a cabin from small blocks of wood.
- Glue a small block of wood ($3/4$" X $3/4$" X $3/4$") next to the mast position to act as a support for the mast. Glue a short piece of dowel to this block and to the deck to form the mast.
- Cut cloth for the sail and fasten craft sticks to the top and bottom of the sail with hot glue. If a helper holds the mast (attached to the boat) flat on the workbench with the boat hanging over the workbench, the yards can be attached to the mast one at a time.
- Other accessories include flags, a little person, a rudder, and I'm sure kids will think of other things.

Film Canister People

- One, two, or three canisters form the body *(Figure 68)* and head.
- Stir sticks or craft sticks make the arms, legs, and feet.
- Use miscellaneous screws, nuts, bolts, and wire for eyes, nose, mouth, and hair.

Figure 67.
A film canister raft.

Figure 68.
A film canister person watching his favorite program.

WOODEN AIRPLANES

Airplanes are interesting projects because children will always come up with variations. Single wing, biplane, triplane. Straight wings or swept back. Windshield or none. *(Figures 69, 70).*

Figure 69. A student-constructed aircraft.

Figure 70. A helicopter.

Tools
- Vice.
- Drill and bits.
- Low-temp hot glue gun and glue sticks.
- Handsaw.
- Eye protection.

Materials
- 2 X 2 for the airplane body 8" to 10" long for each plane. 1 X 2s will work, too.
- Thin strips of wood $1^{1}/2$" wide for the wings and tail. Cut these from scrap 2 X 4s.
- Craft sticks for struts to hold wheels.
- Film canister lids for wheels.
- Scraps of shelf paper or colored tape for decoration. Electrician's tape, which is usually black, also comes in colors and makes great decorations.

Construction
1. Cut the body of the airplane to the desired length.
2. Cut the wings next, and fasten them to the body. Use either hot glue for smaller airplanes or small nails for larger ones.
3. Cut tail pieces and install on the back of the airplane with nails or glue.
4. Decorate.

A "MOM" OR "DAD" SIGN WITH NAIL LETTERING

Making signs with nail lettering was one of those projects that was too complicated and didn't work well at first. Kids liked the idea of making a nail sign, but they had difficulty keeping the nails straight, at a consistent height, and spaced satisfactorily. Often the sign was not recognizable. If I helped with the initial lettering and had children use a spacer, quality improved somewhat, but still success was not what I'd hoped. I realized a pattern would ensure success, so I made patterns for the words "Mom" and "Dad" *(Figure 71).*

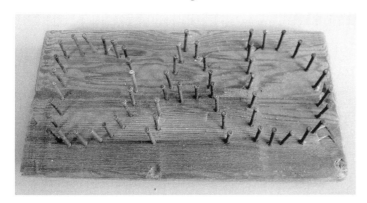

Figure 71.
A "Dad" sign with
nail lettering.

These patterns are just plywood boards (built by a teacher, parent, or volunteer) with holes instead of nails. Children use the patterns by pounding finish nails (with small heads) through the holes. The pattern is then pried off (by an adult) leaving the word outlined in nails. The holes space the nails, keep them the same height and keep them straight. Since it's impossible to have patterns for every child's name I encourage a child to make at least one sign using a pattern before attempting a freehand sign.

Adult Preparation

A parent, teacher, or volunteer makes a pattern (also called a jig).

Tools for the Pattern
- Drill press or hand drill.
- Tape measure.
- $^1/8$" drill bit.
- Square.
- Eye protection.

Materials for the Pattern
- A piece of $^3/4$" plywood about $3^1/2$" X 8" depending how big the word will be.

Pattern Construction
1. Draw the lettering in pencil on the plywood.
2. Lay out the hole positions. There should be about $^3/16$" from the edge of one hole to the edge of the next.
3. Drill $^1/8$" holes at each marked position. A drill press will keep all the holes straight but a hand drill will also work.

Kids: Making the Sign With Nail Lettering

Tools
- Hammer.
- Two medium-sized screwdrivers.

Materials
- A piece of ³/4" plywood a bit larger than the pattern.
- 1¹/4" finish nails. Use finish nails (small heads) only, so the jig can be pried off over the top of the nails.
- Oil or paint for decoration.

Figure 72.
Using the "Mom" jig to make a Mom sign.

Using a Sign Pattern

1. Choose a piece of wood a bit larger than the pattern.
2. Fasten the pattern on top of the wood chosen for the sign by pounding the first two nails in opposite corners of the pattern. *Figure 72* shows the "Mom" pattern in use.
3. Pound a nail in each hole. All the nails should be pounded down so the heads are flush with the top of the pattern. Bent nails should not be pounded over on top of the jig or the jig can't be removed. If a nail starts to bend, I tell kids to stop pounding and go to the next nail. After all the nails are in I'll go back and help pull out the bent ones.
4. Pry the pattern off with the two screwdrivers. After all the nails are in, clamp the sign in the vice and gently pry the pattern off by working around and around the pattern prying a little at a time.

Kids: Making a Sign Without a Pattern

If older kids want to try a sign without a pattern, here is the procedure:

1. Write the lettering in light pencil on the board chosen for the sign.
2. Pound the first nail and then use a spacing stick (a dowel, a pencil or popsicle stick) against it to locate the position for the second nail. Continue the same procedure for the rest of the nails.
3. Sand and oil or paint.

A "DAD" SIGN WITH HOLE LETTERING

The nail sign pattern *(Figure 72)* can be used make a sign of holes, too. Just use the pattern to mark where the holes should be drilled. *Figure 73* shows a "Dad" sign made with holes.

Tools

- Hammer.
- Two screwdrivers.
- Hand drill and ¹/₈" drill bit.
- Eye protection.

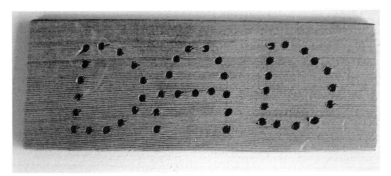

Figure 73.
A "Dad" sign with holes for lettering.

Materials

- One 2" nail.
- A board slightly larger than the pattern.
- Two small nails to hold the pattern in place while marking the hole positions.
- Oil or paint.

Construction

1. Start by fastening the pattern on top of the board with the two small nails.
2. Poke a two-inch nail through hole #1 and tap it a couple times with a hammer. Do the same for all the holes, thus marking where each hole is to be drilled.
3. After the hole positions are marked, remove the pattern.
4. Drill a hole at each marked point. By the time a child has finished this project, he will be fairly competent with the drill.
5. Sand and oil or finish.

MAGIC SIEVE

The magic sieve *(Figure 74)* is shaped like a magnifying glass but instead of glass, it has a piece of window screen. To present this project I ask kids, "What happens when I pour water into this sieve?" The answer, that the water will go right through, is logical, but wrong. This is the sieve that holds water.

After the sieve is constructed, it needs to be dipped in melted wax by an adult, as explained below in step seven.

Figure 74.
Water collects in the magic sieve.

Tools

- Coping saw.
- Hot plate to melt wax (adults only).
- Felt pens.
- Scissors to cut screen.
- A good desk stapler with ¹/4" staples.
- Drill and ¹/4" bit.
- Vice.
- Hammer.
- Eye protection.

Materials

- Paper towels.
- A small pan of candle wax.
- A rubber band.
- A sieve pattern for the kids to trace.
- A piece of ¹/4" or ³/8" plywood 3" wide and 6" long. I've used cedar for this project, too. It is easier to cut but has the disadvantage of splitting easily, which is discouraging, so I switched to plywood.
- A piece of fiberglass screen about 3" square.
- A small measuring cup for pouring water into the sieve.

Construction

1. Trace pattern of the sieve *(Figure 75)* on plywood.
2. Cut out the sieve with a coping saw.
3. Use the coping saw to cut out the big hole in the center of the sieve. Drill a small hole first, then take the blade off the coping saw, insert it through the small hole, reattach the blade, and cut out the big hole.
4. Sand the sieve.
5. Cut out the circle of screen to cover the hole. I cut the screen into 3" squares first. The screen must completely cover the hole and have enough (at least 1/4") left over to staple to the sieve body.
6. Fasten the screen over the hole with the desk stapler. First, give a mini-safety lesson on the use of the stapler. Both hands should remain on top of the stapler. It is important to push down straight, so the stapler won't topple over, exposing a hand to a staple. Use the hammer, if necessary, to make sure the staples are in all the way.
7. Dip the sieve in molten wax.

Safety Note: This step is for an adult only. Molten wax is a fire hazard, an air pollution hazard, and a safety hazard. It should be kept out of the reach of children at all times. Outside is best. Next to an open window with a fan blowing across the wax out the window would be acceptable. I wouldn't do it in a poorly ventilated room. Heat the wax at *a low heat only, just enough to melt it.* After the sieve has been dipped, quickly tap it over a piece of newspaper to knock out any wax caught in the grid. The idea is not to fill the grid with wax, but to coat each wire with wax and leave the grid open. Let the wax dry for a minute or two before testing. I wait until all the sieves are finished, then heat up the wax (standing by it the whole time) and dip them one at a time. As soon as all the sieves have been dipped, I'll remove the molten wax to a safe place while it cools, out of the reach of children.

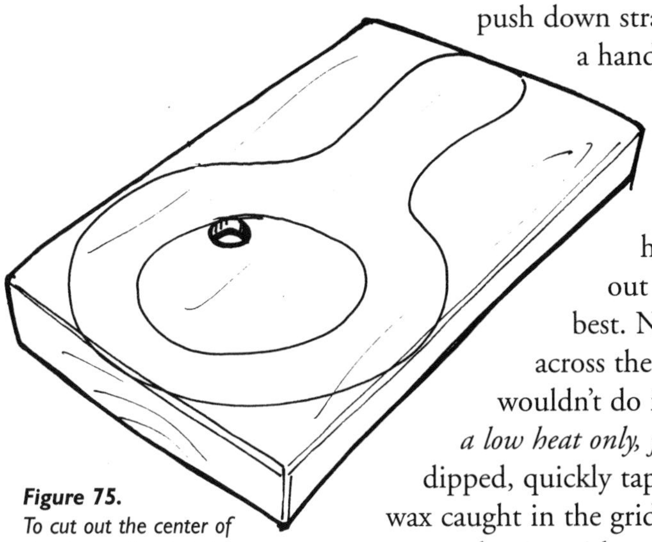

Figure 75.
To cut out the center of the sieve, drill a hole in the sieve and insert the coping saw blade through it.

Using the Sieve

Test the sieve by putting a small (nickel sized) piece of paper towel in the sieve and pouring water slowly and gently onto the towel with a small measuring cup. If you pour directly on to the screen the water will go through, but if you pour on to the paper towel, water will bead up and spread out, filling the sieve. To empty the sieve, touch the underside of the screen with a finger. This breaks the surface tension and allows the water to pour through. When not in use, the sieve should be kept wrapped in a paper towel to protect the wax coating.

CAMERA OBSCURA OR PINHOLE CAMERA

Look through the camera obscura *(Figure 76)* and everything appears upside down! The image is blurred but basic shapes can be recognized. Children enjoy watching each other walk back and forth upside down, or seeing trees upside down.

The key to building the camera obscura is being able to hold the cardboard tube tightly while you cut it. The vice doesn't work well because it crushes the tube before it holds it tight enough to cut. To cut the tube without crushing it, I made a miter box with sides that stick up above the tube.

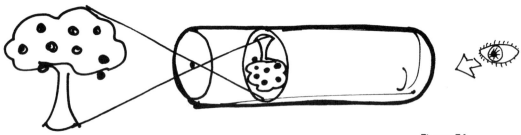

Figure 76.
The camera obscura makes everything look upside down.

Adult Preparation

A parent, teacher, or volunteer needs to make a special miter box to hold the cardboard tube while it's being cut. This miter box is similar to the wooden miter boxes you may have seen in hardware stores, but bigger.

The extra height provides a guide for the saw and allows the tube to be wedged in place while it's cut. This miter box is just three boards fastened together in a U shape (two sides and a bottom) with matching slots cut in the two side boards. The cardboard tube is wedged (with wood scraps) to hold it between the side boards, and the slots guide the saw *(Figure 77)*.

Tools for the Miter Box

- Handsaw.
- Screwdriver.
- Eye protection.
- Vice.
- Try square.
- Drill and bit for predrilling screw holes.

Materials for the Miter Box

- Eight $1^{3/8}$" sheetrock screws.
- Sandpaper.
- Three boards (plywood is good because it won't split) each about 12" long and $3/4$" thick. One 4" wide and the other two 5" wide.

Construction of the Miter Box

1. Fasten the three boards together with screws. The narrow board goes on the bottom between the two uprights. Fasten each board with four screws.
2. Make two saw cuts, one in each side piece, opposite each other and all the way down to the bottom board. These are the slots which will guide the saw.

Figure 77.
The cardboard tube is wedged in the miter box ready to be cut.

Kids: Making a Camera Obscura

Tools

- Handsaw.
- Low-temp hot glue gun and glue sticks.
- Scissors for cutting the tracing paper and aluminum foil.
- Large miter box (above).
- Small nail.

Materials

- 5" square of aluminum foil per project.
- 4" square of tracing paper.
- 3" or 4" diameter cardboard tube from the inside of carpet rolls, about eight inches per project. These can usually be obtained free at carpet stores.
- Electrical tape in various colors.

Construction

1. Use the miter box to cut two cardboard tubes, one 3" long and one about 5" long.
2. Cut a piece of tracing paper to fit between the tubes. I cut squares a bit bigger than the tubes and then let the kids trace and cut the circles themselves; otherwise a lot of paper gets wasted. Glue this circle of tracing paper to one end of the short cardboard tube. Four drops of glue will do it. Try to keep the tracing paper as flat as possible.
3. Glue the two tubes together (another four drops), with the tracing paper between the tubes.
4. Tape the joint with colored electrical tape.
5. Fit a piece of aluminum foil over the short end of the cardboard tube and fasten it with tape. Seal out all the light. Poke a hole in the center of the foil with a nail.
6. Decorate with markers, paint, or colored tape *(Figure 78)*.

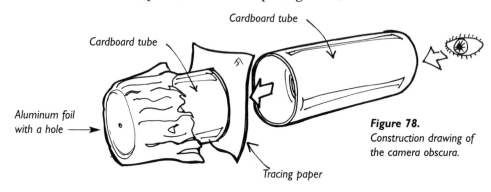

Cardboard tube

Cardboard tube

Aluminum foil
with a hole →

Tracing paper

Figure 78.
Construction drawing of the camera obscura.

Using the Camera Obscura

Do not look directly at the sun! It can damage your eyes. The camera obscura works best on sunny days. Stand in the shade. Hold the camera obscura up to your eye and hold your hands on the joint between your eyes and face, keeping as much light as possible from getting inside the camera obscura.

Look out onto an object that is in the sun. It takes a minute for your eyes to get used to the dark.

First you'll see the sky where the ground should be and vice versa. Then, as your eye adjusts to the dark, you'll pick up more details *(Figure 79)*.

The camera obscura is a classic experiment to illustrate that light travels in a straight line. The image in your eye is upside down just like the image in the camera obscura. Then your brain flips it right side up.

Figure 79.
Kids looking through the camera obscura.

THE MAGNET POST

When I first started working with children I was surprised how many had never played with magnets. As a kid, I spent untold hours experimenting with magnets and I am still intrigued by the magical, invisible lines of force which attract and repel *(Figure 80)*. This project illustrates some of the magnet magic that so intrigued me. I copied the idea from a science catalog that was charging $19.95 for their colored 7-magnet version. I show the kids the catalog advertisement as a lesson in economics as well as in magnets. I think they got as much pleasure as I did from building a $20 item for less than $1.

Tools
- Handsaw.
- Sandpaper.
- Hand drill and ⁵/16" diameter bit to match the dowel.
- Vice.
- Eye protection.

Figure 80.
The magnet post is a good way to introduce children to the magic of magnets.

Materials
- About 3" of 1 X 3 for each project.
- ⁵/16" dowel, about 4¹/2" per project.
- Three (or more) 1" donut magnets per project. Available at hardware stores, from surplus catalogs, or on the internet.
- White glue.

Construction
1. Choose wood for the base and cut a piece approximately 3" X 3".
2. Select dowel and cut about 4¹/2" long. Sand the upper end of the dowel.
3. Drill a hole near the center of the base piece. All the way through is OK.
4. Sand the base piece.
5. Smear a little white glue in the hole and tap the dowel into the hole. Let glue dry.
6. Decorate, put the magnets on the dowel, and watch them float in midair with no visible means of support.

NAIL PUZZLE

The object of the nail puzzle *(Figure 81)* is to balance six nails on top of the standing nail. I usually just show kids how to do it since it is a very hard puzzle to figure out. Kindergartners can learn to do the nail puzzle if they're motivated, although it may take more than one try.

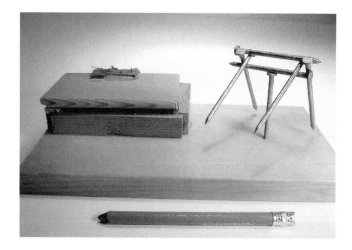

Figure 81.
The nail puzzle.

Tools

- Handsaw.
- Vice.
- Low-temperature hot glue gun and glue sticks.
- Drill and bit slightly smaller than the nails used.
- Sandpaper.
- Hammer.
- Eye protection.

Materials

- 1 X 3, 8" long for each puzzle.
- 7 eight- or tenpenny sized nails. Others will work if they have large heads. Finish nails or siding nails won't work. Nails have sharp points so children need to be cautioned not to poke themselves or others.
- Thin wood strips approximately $1/8$" thick by $3/4$", enough to make boxes to hold the nails.
- Small piece (approximately 1" X 2") of flexible leather for the box hinge.
- Thin piece of wood wide enough for the top of the box.
- Mineral oil or paint.

Construction

1. Select wood for the base. Cut and sand.
2. Drill a hole for the upright nail and pound in, but not so far as to come out the bottom. If the nail protrudes through the base piece, it will scratch any table the nail puzzle is placed on.

3. Select and cut the four thin strips for the nail box sides: two long (longer than the nails) and two short.
4. Assemble the box without glue first to make sure it is big enough to hold the nails. It is easiest to start the box at one corner of the base piece. Fasten it together with hot glue.
5. Decorate.
6. Have kids practice assembling the puzzle several times. It is easy to forget how to do it.

How to Do the Nail Puzzle

The trick is to set all the nails up so they interlock while they are lying flat on the table and then lift them to the top of the standing nail (*Figures 82a, b, and c*).

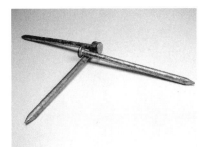
Figure 82a.

Figure 82b.

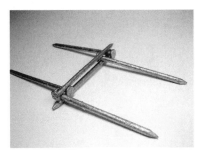
Figure 82c.

1. Lay down one nail.
2. Lay four nails across the first nail. Two are at the head and two at the point as shown.
3. Now lay the last nail on top of the first nail with its head opposite the head of the first nail.
4. Grasp the first and last nails in the center with the thumb and forefinger, pinching the first and last nails together, and balance on top of the standing nail. Another way to do this final balancing act is to use both hands, pinching the top and bottom nails together at either end. *Figure 83* shows Allison excited about putting her nail puzzle together.

Figure 83.
Allison is excited about putting her nail puzzle together.

BOATS

Boats are a favorite project which allow for variation and creativity. They can be sail or power, with a cabin or without, they can float or not, colored or plain. No two boats will be the same .

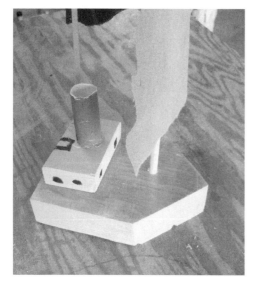

Figure 84.
A sailboat.

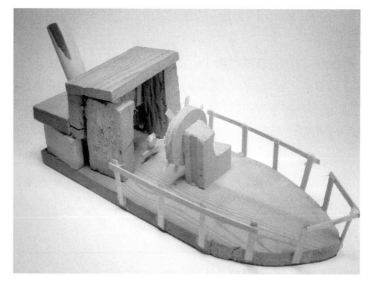

Figure 85.
A power boat.

Tools

- Vice.
- Hacksaw for cutting dowels.
- Sandpaper.
- Scissors for cutting sailcloth.
- Eye protection.
- Handsaw.
- Surform plane.
- Wire cutters for cutting craft sticks.
- Markers for decoration.
- Low-temp hot glue gun and glue sticks.
- Drill with a bit to match the mast size and smaller bit to pre-drill nail holes for attaching cabin.

Materials

- For the boat body, use 1 X 4 or full 1 inch wood, (called $5/4$). The $5/4$ will float a little higher in the water. Make some 1 X 6 and 2 X 4 available too, for nonconformist boats.
- $1/4$" dowels for the mast and/or flag poles.
- Short lengths of thicker dowels $1/2$" or $3/4$" for smoke stacks.
- Multicolored cloth for sails and flags.
- Craft or stir sticks for yards to attach the sails, for rails, or for wheel spokes.
- Miscellaneous small blocks and odd shapes of wood for cabins.

Construction

1. Because hot glue does not hold up in water, boats meant to be used in water should have the cabin nailed instead of fastened with hot glue.
2. Trace the patterns or draw the boat onto the selected wood *(Figure 86)*. I try to have different patterns available, long, short, wide, narrow, pointy bow or rounded bow. The rounded bow is for older kids because it requires the use of a coping saw.

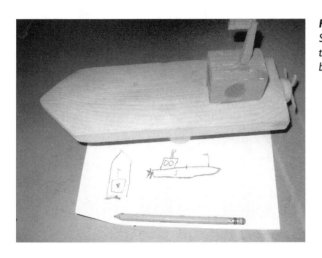

Figure 86.
Some kids like to draw out their own design before beginning construction.

3. Cut out the boat. Because it is considerably easier to use a saw when the blade is vertical (especially when first learning to saw) than when it is at an angle, wood should be placed in the vice so the cut is straight up and down. The wood will be at an angle. This is exactly opposite to our natural tendency to place the wood horizontally and cut at an angle. See *Figure 16*, page 27 for how to set it up.
4. If a mast is desired, I recommend drilling the hole next, as it is sometimes hard to place the boat in the vice for drilling after the cabin, smokestack, and rails have been added. The hole must be deep enough to give support to the dowel. All the way through the boat is OK.
5. Fasten the cabin to the boat. It can be nailed or fastened with hot glue. To fasten the cabin with nails, place the cabin temporarily in the position desired. Draw around it. Remove the cabin and mark the position for two small nails in the cabin footprint, away from the edges. Drill the holes at the marked positions all the way through the bottom of the boat. Flip the boat over (bottom of the boat is facing up) and tap two nails through the holes until they just barely stick out the other side. Place the cabin in position and turn the boat over (upside down again) and, pound the nails in. Children often need help holding the boat and cabin together until the first nail is in.
6. Assemble mast, sail, and yards. Cut the sailcloth (draw it first) to the desired size. Hot glue craft sticks ("yards" in boat parlance) to both the top and the bottom of the sail. Then glue the yards/sail combination to the mast. Put the mast into the boat.
7. Smokestack, sails, flags, railing, etc., come next, with as much or as little detail as each child desires.

BALLOON-POWERED BOAT

Boats like this are available commercially *(Figure 87)*, but here is a simplified version kids can build. I save this project (and the hovercraft) for kids who can blow up their own balloons.

Tools
- Handsaw.
- Eye protection.
- Vice.
- Drill and $^{17}/_{64}$" bit. The purpose of the odd-sized bit is to make a hole the straw will fit through, but not slide out of. $^{1}/_{4}$" was just a bit tight for my straws. Check your straw size and get the appropriate bit. Alternately, you could ream a $^{1}/_{4}$" hole out with a piece of sandpaper.
- Balloon pump for kids who can't blow up a balloon.
- Small scissors with a sharp point for cutting one end of the straw lengthwise.

Materials
- Wood for the boat. 1 X 4 about 8" long.
- $^{3}/_{4}$" length of $^{3}/_{4}$" dowel. A chunk of old broom handle will work.

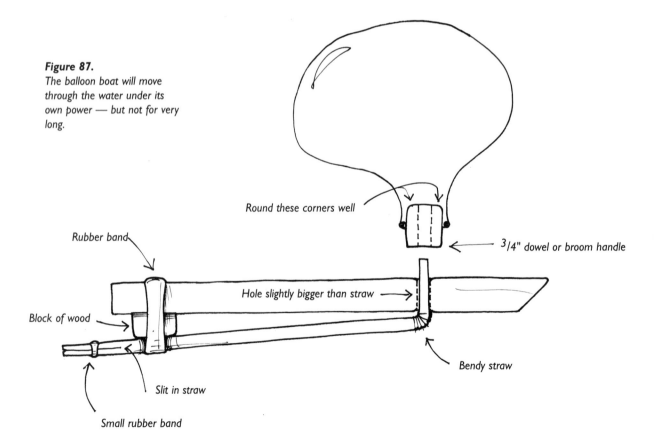

Figure 87.
The balloon boat will move through the water under its own power — but not for very long.

- A big balloon.
- Two short, strong rubber bands. About 2" long X $^{1}/_{4}$" wide.
- One very small rubber band.
- A small block of wood about $^{1}/_{2}$" X 1" X 1".
- Two small nails to fasten the above block to the bottom of the boat.
- A flexible straw.
- A small amount of waterproof glue. I use yellow carpenter's glue that says "waterproof" on the label.
- Miscellaneous wood for cabins, dowels for flagpoles, and cloth for flags.
- A tub of water for testing the boat.

Construction

1. Cut out the boat. Check Boats, page 104 if you want more details. Sand.
2. Drill a $^{17}/_{64}$" hole on the centerline, about a third of the way back from the bow.
3. Cut a section of $^{3}/_{4}$" dowel (or broom handle) $^{3}/_{4}$" long. Sand the upper edge of this dowel with sandpaper until it's very smooth. The balloon fits over this dowel so any slivers on this edge will pop the balloon.
4. Carefully drill a $^{17}/_{64}$" hole through the dowel.
5. Nail the small block of wood on the underside of the boat near the stern. This block will keep the end of the straw under water and allow steering adjustments.
6. Make the hole at the underwater end of the straw smaller so the air won't come out so fast. Do this by making a 2" slit at the end of the straw. Then wrap a small rubber band around the slit. I closed my straw down to about $^{1}/_{16}$", but you should encourage kids to experiment.
7. Assembly: Poke the straw up through the hole in the boat so it sticks up about $^{1}/_{2}$". Put glue on the end of the straw and the bottom of the dowel. Slide the dowel over the straw. Use one of the thick rubber bands to hold the dowel against the boat until the glue dries. Use the second rubber band around the stern of the boat to hold the end of the straw tight against the block under the boat.
8. Blow up the balloon and slip it over the dowel while still keeping it pinched off so no air will escape. Place the boat in a tub of water and let go of the balloon. The boat should cruise under its own power. If the tub is large enough, you can aim the straw to one side and the boat will travel in a circle.
9. Add a cabin, flags, smokestack, etc., to the boat as desired.

HOVERCRAFT

This hovercraft *(Figure 88)* is a phonograph record that glides above the surface of a table, supported by a thin cushion of air from a balloon. A demonstration of the model will ensure enthusiastic builders. Push the hovercraft across the table. See how it sticks? Now inflate the balloon and slip it over the dowel. Give the hovercraft a gentle push and watch how it glides. Kids should be able to blow up their own balloon or you can buy a balloon pump. Sometimes I couple this project with the fire drill to illustrate opposites. The hovercraft results in very little friction between the bottom of the record and the table. The fire drill is an example of lots of friction—which results in heat.

Figure 88.
Some clever kid copied a popular superhero for his hovercraft.

Tools

- Sandpaper.
- Vice.
- Keyhole saw.
- Hand drill and $1/8$" drill bit.
- Low-temp hot glue gun and glue sticks.
- Eye protection.

Materials

- A 10" or larger balloon. A balloon pump is handy for younger kids so they can blow up their own balloon.
- A $3/4$" length of $3/4$" diameter dowel. A broom or mop handle will work.
- An old 33 rpm record. Usually these are available free from used record stores. The records can be scratched but not warped. Site along the bottom of the record to make sure it is flat. Get extra records.

Construction *(Figure 89)*

1. Sand the paper label off around the hole on the record (to an area about the size of a quarter). This allows the dowel to be glued directly to the plastic, not to the paper.

2. Cut the dowel or broom handle piece $3/4$" long, or a bit longer. Better too long than too short. Too short and the balloon won't stay on. When cutting the dowel, a common mistake is to press down too hard on the saw. This splits a small splinter off the dowel making it so the balloon won't seal properly.

3. Sand the corners of the dowel thoroughly so the slivers will not pop the balloon. I tell children the dowel should be as smooth as the model.

4. Put the short dowel in the vice and drill a $1/8$" hole all the way through its center.

5. Glue the sanded dowel (with the hole) to the record. Be sure to place the hole in the dowel over the hole in the record. Use plenty of glue, but not so much as to plug the hole. Build up a fillet of glue around the outside of the dowel for extra reinforcement.

6. Check the hole to be sure it isn't filled with glue. If it is, run the drill through the hole again to clear it out. This can be done by flipping the hovercraft over and placing the dowel in the vice and then running the drill through the hole from the record side.

7. Test flight. A linoleum floor makes a good test path. A smooth table will also work but has the problem of hovercrafts flying off the table onto the floor. The hovercraft will not work on a carpet or a rough (cement, for example) floor. The surface must be smooth and clean. Have kids sweep the floor before the test. Blow up the balloon, slip it over the dowel, and give the hovercraft a gentle shove.

Some kids can blow the balloon up but can't quite keep the air from escaping while they slip the end of the balloon over the dowel. I help them. The hovercraft should glide across the floor.

8. Decorate.

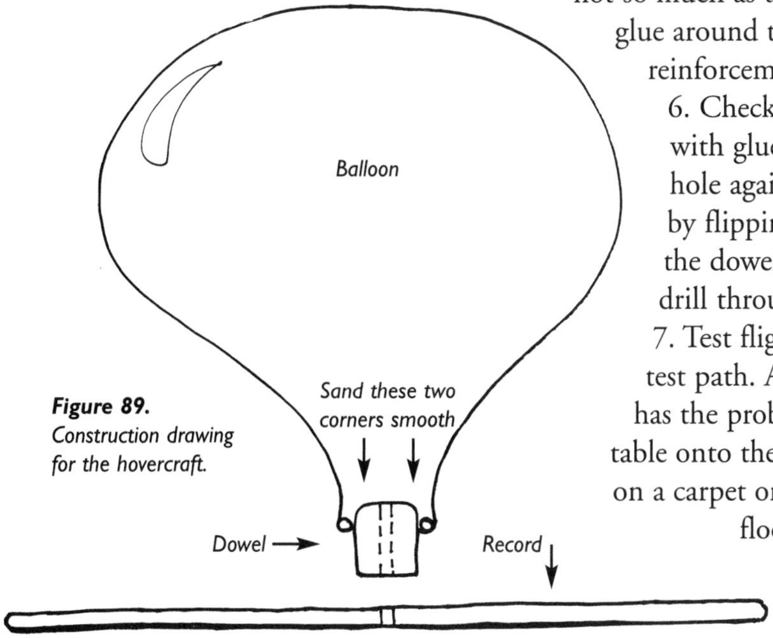

Figure 89.
Construction drawing for the hovercraft.

Balloon

Sand these two corners smooth

Dowel →   *Record* ↓

Troubleshooting

Every once in a while a hovercraft won't work. One common problem is a hole plugged with hot glue. Check to make sure the hole is clear. If air from the balloon is coming out underneath the record, and it still doesn't work, the record is probably warped and will have to be replaced. Usually the dowel can be broken off the defective record (tap it with a block of wood) and put on a new one.

TIC-TAC-TOE

For several years I had a tic-tac-toe *(Figure 90)* set for kids to copy, but not many sets were built. The problem was that children had difficulty laying out the hole positions. Even though I repeatedly demonstrated how to use the tape and square, it was still too confusing. Looking back, I can see this was a classic example of expecting too much. A jig (or pattern) helped to keep all the holes in the right place for the sign-making project so I built one for the tic-tac-toe set. The tic-tac-toe jig is just a board with small (1/8") holes drilled completely through at the nine peg positions. This jig is temporarily tacked to the child's board and the hole positions transferred to the child's wood. With hole positions marked accurately, it's not too difficult to keep the larger holes aligned .

Adult Preparation

A parent, teacher, or volunteer needs to make the jig.

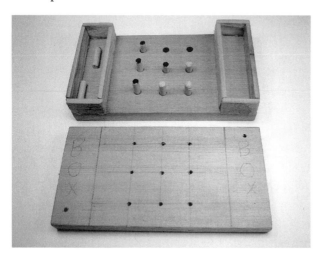

Figure 90.
The tic-tac-toe set (on top) and the jig used to make it.

Tools for the Jig
- Handsaw.
- 1/8" drill bit.
- Square.
- Eye protection.
- Sandpaper.
- Tape measure.
- Square.
- A 2" or 2 1/2" nail.
- Vice.
- A hand drill will work if you're careful, but a drill press will be easier and more accurate. Any inaccuracies made will be repeated each time a child uses the jig.

Materials for the Jig
- Sandpaper.
- 3/4" plywood at least 3 1/2" square. The jig shown in *Figure 90* is about 7" long.

Construction of the Jig

1. Cut the wood to size and lay out the position of the holes. The holes are 1" apart and 3/4" from the side of the jig.
2. To help center the drill bit, make a small indentation at each hole position with a nail. Drill 1/8" holes all the way through the plywood.
3. Drill two holes at opposite corners of the jig.
4. Sand the jig.

Kids: Making the Tic-Tac-Toe Set

Tools

- Handsaw.
- Miter block (Appendix, page 187).
- Low-temp hot glue gun and glue sticks.
- Vice.
- Hand drill or hand-operated drill press and 5/16" drill bit.
- Square.
- Hammer and nail.
- Eye protection.
- Sandpaper.

Materials

- Piece of wood approx. 3/4" X 31/2" X 7".
- Two nails about 11/2" long.
- About 20" of thin wood strips 3/4" X 1/8" for a box to contain the pegs.
- Two colors of paint for painting tops of dowels. Markers will also work.
- 12" of 1/4" dowel for pegs.
- Oil or paint for decoration.

Construction

1. Choose a piece of wood for the board. Center the jig on top of the board and temporarily tack it in place with small nails *(Figure 91)* through two corner holes.
2. Place the wood, with the jig nailed on top, in the vice. Poke the nail through each jig hole and tap it two or three times to mark the hole positions in the project board.
3. Once hole positions are marked, remove the jig and drill 5/16" holes at each position. To keep track of the hole depth without removing the drill, place a piece of tape around the drill bit 3/8" from the end of the bit. Drilling to the tape will keep all the holes about 3/8" deep.
4. Use the thin strips and the hot glue gun to construct a box (for holding the pegs) at each end of the board. See page 119 for box construction.
5. Use the miter block to cut ten dowels, five for each side, about 3/4" long.
6. Paint the tops of five dowels one color and the tops of the other five another color. Decorate the board.

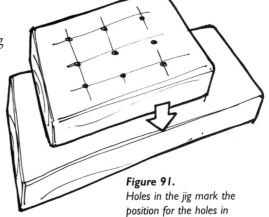

Figure 91.
Holes in the jig mark the position for the holes in the project.

NAIL BOARD

The nail board is a board with ten rows of ten nails spaced at 1" intervals. Children use rubber bands to connect the tops of the nails, making different shapes and designs *(Figure 92)*. I've also heard this called a geoboard.

At one of my workshops, a teacher saw the jigs I used for making the Mom and Dad nail signs and suggested using the same type of jig so kids could make their own nail boards. It was a great idea and turned out to be a very popular project. Some people have trouble visualizing how the jig is used. This jig is just a board, a guide really, with holes in the exact place the nails will go on the project itself. Pounding nails through the holes in the jig spaces the nails correctly (saving all the measuring and layout) and keeps them all at the same height. After all the nails are in, the jig is pried off (it can be used over and over), leaving the nail board with the nails in nice, even rows.

Adult Preparation

A teacher, parent, or volunteer needs to make the jig.

Figure 92.
The idea for making a nail board came from a teacher in one of my woodworking workshops.

Tools for the Jig

- Handsaw.
- $1/8$" drill bit.
- Vice.
- A square for laying out hole positions.
- A drill of some sort. A drill press makes the job easy (and the jig more accurate) by keeping the holes straight, but a hand drill (electric, battery, or egg beater type) will also work. If you drill all these holes by hand, you'll be pretty good with a hand drill by the time you're done.

- Sandpaper.
- Tape measure.
- Eye protection.

Materials for the Jig

- 12" X 12" piece of $3/4$" plywood.

Construction of the Jig

1. Put marks at 1" intervals down adjacent sides of the 12" square board. Use the square to draw straight and parallel lines across the board at each mark. This should result in a board divided into 1" squares.
2. Drill holes at the point where the lines cross. Sand the splinters and the corners and you're finished.

Kids: Building the Nail Board

Tools

- Hammer.
- Sandpaper.
- Two slotted screwdrivers.
- Handsaw.
- Surform plane.
- Low-temp hot glue gun and glue sticks.
- Eye protection.
- Vice.

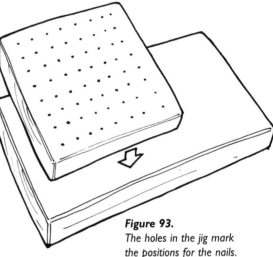

Materials

- One 12" X 14" X $3/4$" thick plywood.
- $1^1/4$" finish nails (with the small heads). 100 nails, plus a few extras, for each board.
- About 12" of $3/16$" ($1/4$" or $1/8$" will work) X $1^1/2$" wood strips to make a small box to hold rubber bands. See page 119 for box instructions.
- Lots of colored rubber bands of various lengths.

Figure 93.
The holes in the jig mark the positions for the nails.

Construction

1. Cut out a board 12" X 14". Sand.
2. Place the jig on top, and at one end, of the board. Align three sides of the jig with three sides of the board *(Figure 93)*.
3. Pound nails in opposite corners of the jig to hold it in place. Once the jig is in place, pound nails into the rest of the holes. Pound the nails down even with the top of the jig. Caution children not to bend the nails over on top of the jig as it will prevent the jig from being removed. If a nail starts to bend, stop and remove it. Start another nail. Sometimes after a child has finished pounding, I have to come back and pry out a few bent-over nails before the jig will come off.
4. Once all the nails are in, place the nail board in a vice and pry the jig off the top of the nail board, using the two slotted screwdrivers. This is usually a job for an adult. Try to do most of the prying against the jig so the nail board will not be marked up.
5. Make a box to hold the rubber bands. Cut four pieces for the box sides: Two pieces 4" long and two pieces 2" long. Glue them in place, one piece at a time.

CAMP STOOL

Few can guess what the camp stool *(Figure 94)* is the first time they see it. Most are amused when they find out. A child's legs provide the second and third legs for this single leg stool. The seat can be a slice from a tree, which requires adult preparation (see below) or a chunk of 2 X 6, which is easier to find.

Adult Preparation

A parent, teacher, or volunteer needs to prepare the tree slices. Find trees or branches 4" to 5" in diameter. Paint the ends and let them dry for a few months to help prevent cracking as explained in the section on wood, page 52. Cut the branches into 2" slices with a chain saw or band saw. A band saw will leave a smoother cut. Sometimes you can find tree sections that aren't cracked too badly in a firewood pile. Neighbors who are trimming trees are another good source.

Kids: Making the Camp Stools

Figure 94.
The camping stool in use.

Tools

- Handsaw.
- Vice.
- Brace with bit to match the dowel or broom handle. Or hand-operated drill press.
- White glue or yellow carpenter's glue. Hot glue won't work.
- Hammer.
- Eye protection.

Materials

- A 1 1/2" thick slice from a tree about 4" to 6" in diameter. 2" lumber of the same dimensions will also work.
- 10" of 3/4" dowel or broom handle for the stool leg. Dowels and drill bits vary in their actual measurements, so make sure the dowel is a tight fit into the hole made by the 3/4" bit. Drill a test hole ahead of time.
- 5" square of 3/8" or 1/2" plywood for each stool.
- Six or eight nails (screws could be used) about 1 1/2" long for each project. Make sure they don't go all the way through the seat.
- A plastic cap to fit the end of the dowel leg. I've also used colored electrician's tape.

Construction

1. Sand the top of the seat. If you are using lumber instead of a tree slice, rounding the corners is a nice touch.

2. Cut the corners off the 5" plywood square so they don't stick out, and fasten it with glue and nails to the bottom (the unsanded side) of the seat. Put the nails into the plywood piece before stacking it on top of the seat to finish nailing. This piece will hold the seat together in case it splits and will provide a thicker base for the stool leg. Pre-drilling the six holes in the plywood piece will make the nailing easier *(Figure 95)*.

3. Drill a hole with the brace and bit (or hand-operated drill press) 1" deep in the center of the bottom of the stool. The dowel must fit snugly into the hole.

4. Cut the dowel or broom handle about 10" long for the leg. Cover the inside of the hole with glue and tap the dowel into the hole with a hammer. Let the glue dry.

5. Put the rubber cap (or colored tape) on the stool leg and test your stool.

6. The hardest part of this project for children is drilling the 3/4" hole. For the younger children, I'll help by setting up a station where I hold the brace horizontally (it's easier to turn), and have the child rotate the handle.

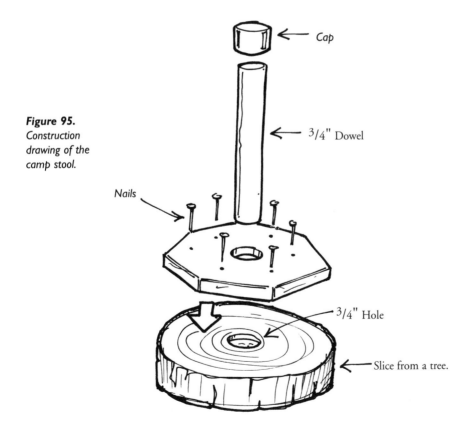

Figure 95.
Construction drawing of the camp stool.

Cap

3/4" Dowel

Nails

3/4" Hole

Slice from a tree.

MR. BEE

Mr. Bee is built from paper, wood, popsicle-sticks, string, and a rubber band. When whirled in a circle, the paper bee acts like a wind vane to keep the rubber band at right angles to the air. The rubber band vibrates like a guitar string and sounds like a bee. Several Mr. Bees whirled at the same time sound like a swarm of bees *(Figure 96)*.

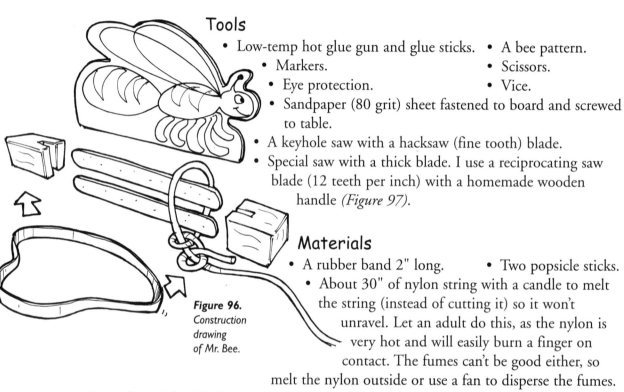

Tools

- Low-temp hot glue gun and glue sticks.
- Markers.
- Eye protection.
- Sandpaper (80 grit) sheet fastened to board and screwed to table.
- A keyhole saw with a hacksaw (fine tooth) blade.
- Special saw with a thick blade. I use a reciprocating saw blade (12 teeth per inch) with a homemade wooden handle *(Figure 97)*.
- A bee pattern.
- Scissors.
- Vice.

Figure 96.
Construction drawing of Mr. Bee.

Materials

- A rubber band 2" long.
- About 30" of nylon string with a candle to melt the string (instead of cutting it) so it won't unravel. Let an adult do this, as the nylon is very hot and will easily burn a finger on contact. The fumes can't be good either, so melt the nylon outside or use a fan to disperse the fumes.
- Two popsicle sticks.
- Piece of wood 3/4" X 3/4" about 2" long for blocks to hold the ends of the popsicle sticks.
- A small piece (2 1/2" X 3 1/2") of stiff paper. I use file folders or card stock.

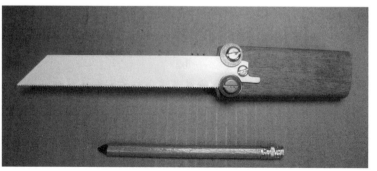

Figure 97.
A homemade saw with a thick blade.

Construction

1. Make two blocks (³/₄" X ³/₄") with ³/₈" deep slots. Mark the 2" X ³/₄" X ³/₄" piece for length and slot position. Cut the slot first by placing the wood in the vice vertically, that is, with the length of the wood up and down. Cut the slot with the wide saw blade or run the wide blade through the cut after using the keyhole saw. Switch the wood to the horizontal position and cut the block to length with the keyhole saw. Cut the second block in the same manner. Sand the blocks *(Figure 98)*.

2. Fit the popsicle sticks to the slots. This is tricky. If the slot isn't wide enough and the sticks are forced into it, the block will split. If the sticks don't slide into the slots easily, widen the slot by running the fat saw through it again, or by sanding the sticks. If you choose sanding, hold the end of the stick nearly flat, and move back and forth on a piece of sandpaper.

3. Glue the two popsicle sticks into the blocks. Put the block on the glue-table, slot facing up, and show kids how to hold it down with a popsicle stick, not fingers. Squirt hot glue into the slot and slide the two sticks into the glue-filled slot. Do the same for the second block, which results in two popsicle sticks with a block glued at each end.

4. Trace the bee pattern on the card stock, cut it out, and draw/color a bee. Glue this bee to the flat sides of the two popsicle sticks.

5. Tie the string around one end of the popsicle sticks next to the block. Two overhand knots or two half hitches are good. See *Figure 96,* page 116. Often a knot-tying lesson is necessary. Put hot glue over the top of the knot so it won't come undone.

6. The last step is to put the rubber band on without any twists. After the rubber band is on, you're ready for a test flight. Kids will be excited and it is necessary to make sure they don't stand too close to each other when playing with Mr. Bee.

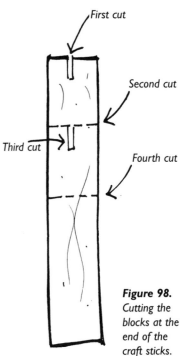

First cut

Second cut

Third cut

Fourth cut

Figure 98.
Cutting the blocks at the end of the craft sticks.

Troubleshooting

If Mr. Bee doesn't work, most often it is because there is a twist in the rubber band. Occasionally someone will make the paper bee too small. It must be large enough to act as a wind vane to keep the rubber band parallel to the wind. After Mr. Bee has been used for a while, the string becomes twisted. I show kids how to hold the bee, letting the string run free, and run their fingers down the string to take the twists out of the string.

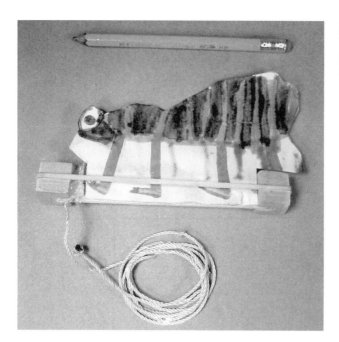

Figure 99.
This guy could use wings, but still flies (and buzzes) well.

THE BASIC BOX

This box is the simplest box I could figure out how to make. It is put together with hot glue so it is easier than a box put together with nails or screws. It's made, top, bottom, and sides, from thin strips of 2 X 4. The hinge is leather and is fastened with hot glue. Once kids go through the steps of building this box, they can alter the dimensions and fastenings to make planters, tool boxes, or any other box. Boxes make great presents for Mom and Dad *(Figure 100a and b)*.

Adult Preparation

A parent, teacher, or volunteer needs to cut the box sides ($^3/16$" thick strips) from 2 X 4s or any 2" material using a table saw.

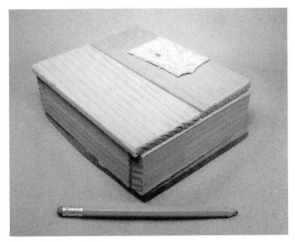

Figure 100a and b.
The basic box (a) and basic box with the lid open (b).

Kids: Building the Box

Tools

- Handsaw.
- Keyhole saw with hacksaw blade.
- Low-temp hot glue gun and glue sticks.
- Vice.
- Eye protection.
- Sandpaper.
- Miter block. In order to make the box corners fit together, kids must be able to make straight cuts. For younger kids, a miter block is essential for success. See page 187.
- Decoration materials: marking pens, paint, shelf paper. Although I like the natural wood finish, many kids prefer to paint their boxes.

Materials

- Thin strips of wood $1^1/2$" wide X $^3/16$" thick for box sides.
- A few narrower strips of wood also $^3/16$" thick for the bottom and top of box.
- Small scrap pieces of leather (2" X 2") for hinges.

Construction

1. Box sides come from long precut strips so I demonstrate how to measure the first piece against the model *(Figure 101)*. Once the first piece is cut, use it as a pattern to mark the other three sides as shown in *Figure 102*. Sand each piece. Kids may try marking the pattern length on the precut strip four times before cutting. It seems like a good idea, but doesn't work. Because each pencil mark and each saw cut will be a little off, inaccuracies compound, resulting in four pieces of different lengths. Measuring with a tape at 4", 8", 12" and 16" and then going back and cutting won't work either. Each pencil mark and each cut will be slightly off, and errors will compound.

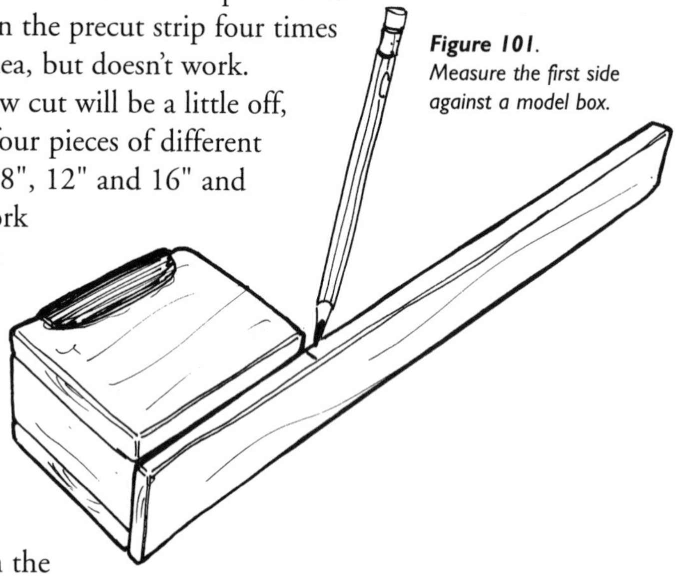

Figure 101.
Measure the first side against a model box.

2. Make sure opposite sides of a rectangular box are the same length by holding them stacked together with one edge on the workbench. If they aren't the same, I'll hold them together in the miter block, with the shortest on top, and the student can quickly even them up all at once.

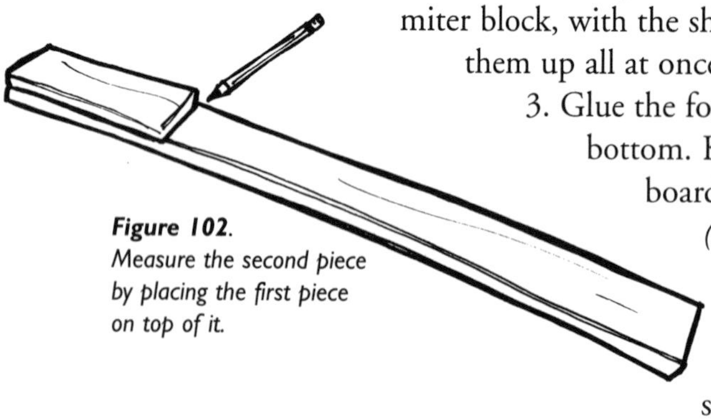

Figure 102.
Measure the second piece by placing the first piece on top of it.

3. Glue the four sides together, to make a box with no top or bottom. Kids may surprise you with the number of ways four boards can be glued together so demonstrate how to do it *(Figure 103)*. Put glue on the end grain of one board and attach it to the flat surface of an adjacent board. Keep both pieces flat on the workbench. Repeat this procedure with a second side. This should result in three pieces glued together in a U shape. Next, put glue on the two ends of the U and fasten the fourth side of the box together. This should form a box with four sides but no top or bottom.

Figure 103.
Assemble the four sides to make a box with no top or bottom.

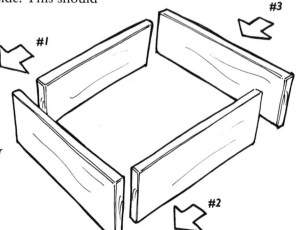

4. Make the box bottom and lid. Cut pieces to fit the bottom *(Figure 104)* and glue them on one at a time to the bottom of the box. The last piece might have to be cut lengthwise or maybe some combination of 1^1/2" and narrower strips will completely cover the bottom. Just as for the bottom, cut pieces to cover the top of the box. Put these pieces, good side down, on the workbench and hot glue them together with two cross strips cut from the thin material. These thin strips should be a little shorter than the lid so they will fit inside the box as the lid closes.

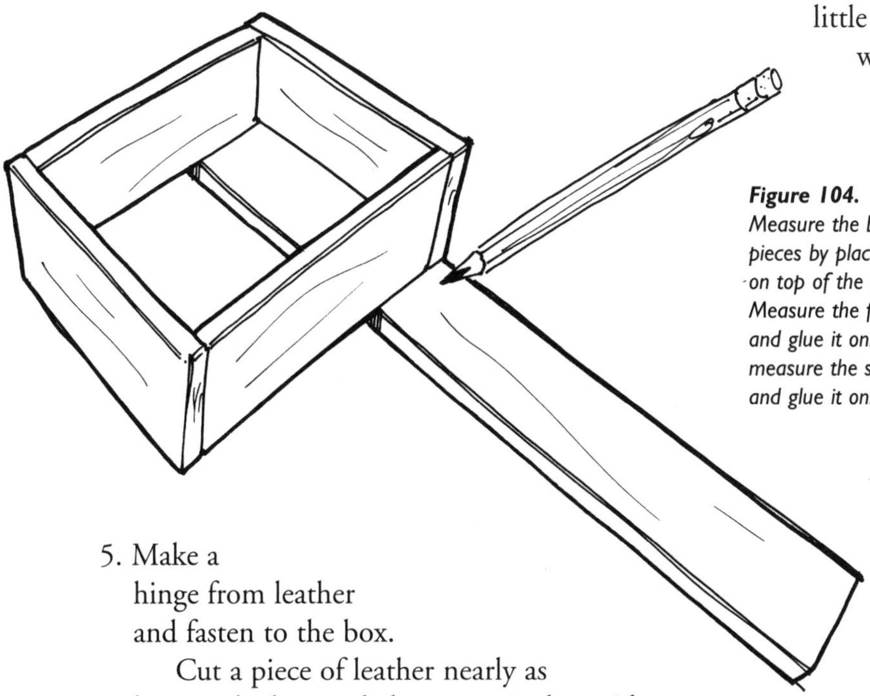

Figure 104.
Measure the bottom pieces by placing the box on top of the material. Measure the first piece and glue it on. Then measure the second piece and glue it on.

5. Make a hinge from leather and fasten to the box.

   Cut a piece of leather nearly as long as the box and about two inches wide. Most of the time I precut the leather.

   Here is how to fasten the hinge on. Fold the hinge in half and crease it. Above the crease will go on the lid and below the crease will go on the box side. Glue the bottom half of the hinge to the box first. Do this in stages. Put some glue down on the box and press the leather into it. The glue will be warm through the leather but won't burn. Work around the rest of the hinge with more glue to make sure it is held down at the edges. Wait 30 seconds or so until the glue dries, put the lid on the box, fold the hinge over it, and go through the same procedure with the top part of the hinge, gluing a little at a time. Try not to get glue between the box and the lid or the box will be glued shut.

TOOL OR PLANTER BOX

If you take the handle off the tool box pictured in *Figure 105* you have a planter. Boxes are great projects because once the idea of how to make a box is understood, dimensions can be altered to fit just about any situation.

Hot glue will not be strong enough for this box. Nails or screws are necessary. Otherwise, it is built much the same as the basic box. Most often nails are strong enough, but for a super strong box, use screws. Before building one of these larger boxes, read the sections on fastening two boards together (pages 60-62), nails and screws (page 58), and on countersinking (page 63).

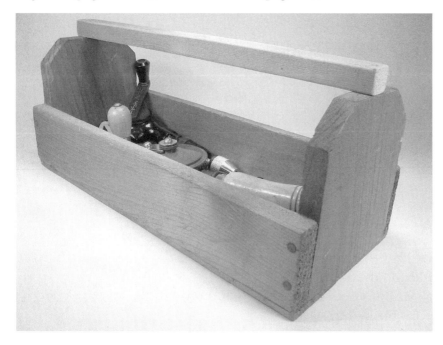

Figure 105.
With slight alterations, it could be a planter or storage box.

Tools

- Handsaw.
- Eye protection.
- Hand drill and proper sized bit to pre-drill nail or screw holes.
- Countersink or nail set.
- Vice.

Materials

- 1 X 4 for the box sides, about 32".
- 1³/8" sheetrock screws to hold the handle.
- ³/4" nails to attach the box bottom.
- A strip of 1" material 16" long for the handle.
- 1 X 6 for the box ends, about 12".
- 1¹/4" nails for the box corners.
- ¹/8" plywood for the bottom of the box.

Construction

1. Cut the sides of the box. Two 16" 1 X 4s for the sides. Two 6" 1 X 6s for the ends. I cut the corners off the 1 X 6s to give the ends of the box a more finished appearance.
2. Fasten the sides together with nails or screws. This results in a box with no top or bottom.
3. Make the box bottom. Plywood is good because it's light and big enough to cover the bottom in one piece. Several smaller strips would work, too. Set the open box in a corner of the bottom material and trace around both the inside and outside of the box sides. Put matching numbers, one on the box and one on the bottom, to remind which side of the bottom matches which side of the box.
4. Cut the bottom out.
5. Mark on the bottom piece where the nails will go, halfway between the edge of the wood and the lines marking the inside of the box.
6. Put the bottom piece in the vice and pre-drill the nail holes at each marked spot.
7. Turn the box upside down, hold the bottom on, (matching the numbers) and nail in place. It is hard to hold and nail at the same time, so often I'll hold the pieces together for a child until a couple of nails are in.

FIRE DRILL

I found this project in an old Scout Handbook. The book tells how to make a fire drill using a branch, a shoelace, and your trusty scout knife in case you get lost in the woods.

Caution: Adult Supervision Required

Although it is unlikely, wood can smolder and burst into flames long after anyone would expect it to. To make sure this does not happen, dip any charred wood into a bucket of water. Also, a determined student can actually drill (burn) through a board with this tool, so be sure to have an extra board to protect any tabletop. Students should wear goggles to protect their eyes in case the drill flips out toward their face *(Figure 106)*.

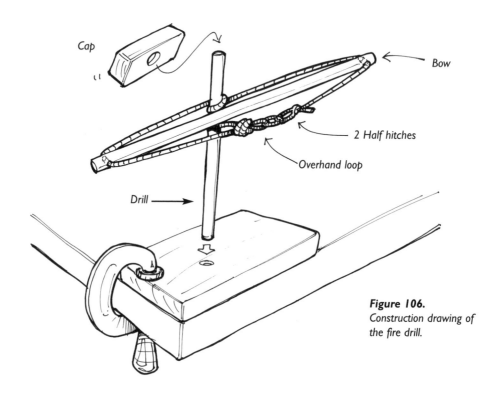

Figure 106.
Construction drawing of the fire drill.

Tools

- Keyhole saw with a hacksaw blade.
- Hand drill with a $1/8$" bit.
- Surform plane.
- Hand pencil sharpener.
- A clamp to keep base piece from moving.
- $3/8$" or $5/16$" drill bit for making indentations in handle and base.
- Vice.
- Soldering iron or candle.
- Sandpaper.
- Small triangular file.

Materials

- A 3/8" dowel (or straight branch) about 16" long. This will be the bow.
- Another 3/8" dowel about 8" long. This is the drill.
- Three feet of 3/32" nylon line for the bow string. Nylon is better than cotton because it will stretch and stay tight around the drill.
- 1 X 4 cedar about 10" long. This will be the base piece of wood that smokes.
- A small block of hardwood approximately 3/4" thick, 1" wide and 3" long. Actual dimensions aren't important. Its function is to hold and steady the top of the drill.
- A bucket of water to soak the smoldering wood in after using the fire drill.

Construction

1. Cut the bow 16" long and the drill 8" long using the keyhole saw. Taper both ends of the drill just a little (not to a sharp point) with the pencil sharpener. This slight taper will help keep the drill centered in the base board and handle indentations as it spins.

2. With the large drill bit, begin a few indentations, 1/8" deep, in the base piece. These will also help keep the drill in place as it spins. Drill an indentation in the center of the top handle piece, too.

3. Using the Surform plane, round the corners, then sand and smooth the top handle piece so it's comfortable to hold.

4. Drill two small holes for the bow string, one at each end of the bow. A drill bit tends to slip off a round object so here is a trick that will give the bit a place to start: make two shallow cuts with a file, crossing each other, in the shape of an X, and start the bit in the center of the X.

5. Attach the bowstring to the bow. Tie a loop in one end of the string by doubling it and

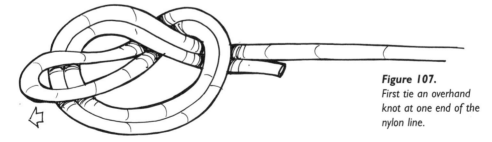

Figure 107.
First tie an overhand knot at one end of the nylon line.

tying an overhand knot *(Figure 107)*. Thread the other end through the two holes of the bow and back to the loop. Tie it with two half hitches. See *Figure 96*, page 116 for how to tie two half hitches. Tension is critical. The string should be tight but not super tight. If the string is too loose, it won't turn the drill. If it's too tight, it won't fit around the drill.

Using the Fire Drill

The bottom of the drill (where smoke will appear) should be roughed up with sandpaper before beginning. Insert the drill under the string and rotate it 180 degrees so the string goes around the drill. *Figures 108a, b, and c* show how to wrap the bow string around the drill. The drill should end up at right angles to the bow. Be careful, as the drill will flip out and fly across the room if you release it. Put the bottom of the drill into one of the pre-drilled indentations on the base piece and the top of the drill into the handle indentation. Hold the drill upright between the handle and the base, press down on the handle just a little, and move the bow back and forth, gently at first, to get the rhythm. As the bow moves back and forth, the line around the drill should rotate the drill even after increasing the pressure on the top handle. If the line slips around the drill instead of turning it, undo the half hitches and tighten the bowstring.

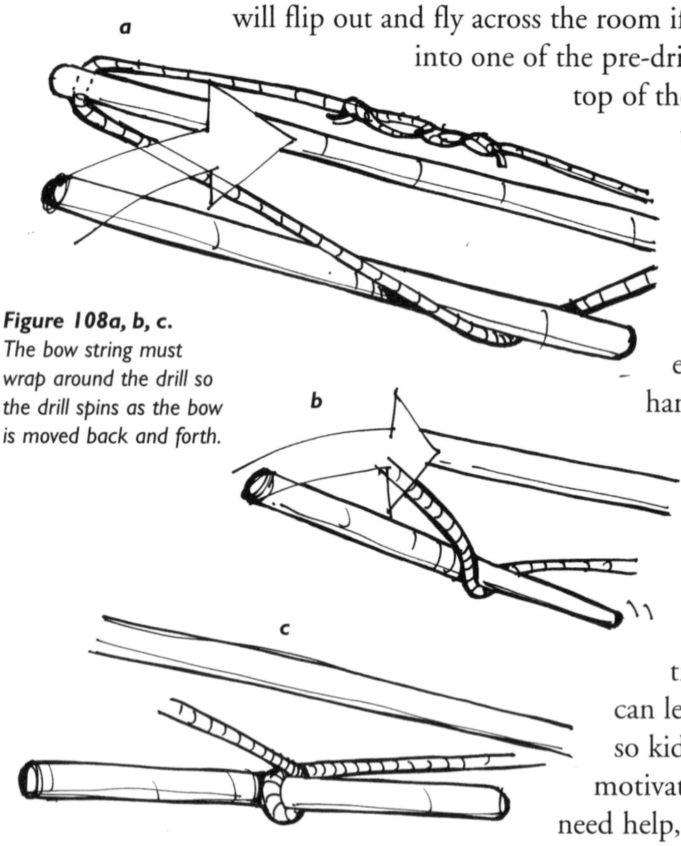

Gradually increase downward pressure on the top handle. To produce smoke, the drill must move rapidly back and forth for 15 seconds or so. This is a tricky tool to use but 3rd and 4th graders can learn if they're motivated. I demonstrate first so kids realize it works. A demonstration also motivates children to try it themselves. If they need help, I'll hold the top handle for them and/or hold the other end of the bow and help move it faster.

Too much pressure on the drill and it won't spin. Not enough pressure and it won't create smoke. Sometimes it is easier if two kids work together. One can hold the drill upright with both hands, bracing her elbows on the table, while the other moves the bow back and forth. The part of the drill dowel that goes in the top handle should wear into a hard, smooth surface. Sometimes it smokes, too.

Figure 108a, b, c.
The bow string must wrap around the drill so the drill spins as the bow is moved back and forth.

PERSONAL PING-PONG

This mini ping-pong table consists of a small board (the table) with a handle and a "net" *(Figure 109)*. The idea is to bounce the ball from one side of the net to the other by gently twisting the handle back and forth. I learned about this project from a woman who built and sold them at craft fairs. She lured customers by keeping the ball in play for minutes at a time. It is easier to build than to play, but since you play against yourself, you always win!

Tools
- Handsaw.
- Tape measure and square.
- Eye protection.
- Low-temperature hot glue gun and glue sticks.
- Vice.
- Hand drill and bit for pre-drilling screws.

Materials
- 1 X 2 about a foot long for the handle.
- Ping-pong ball.
- Green paint.
- White glue.
- $1/4$" plywood approximately 6" X 12" for the table.
- Two $3/4$" screws to fasten the plywood to the handle.
- 14" of thin ($1/8$") wood about $1 1/2$" wide for the "net" and a container to hold the ball.

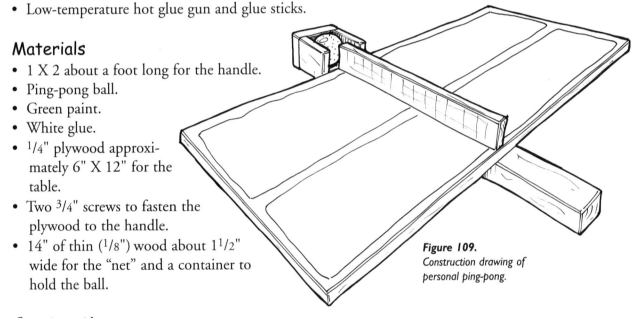

Figure 109.
Construction drawing of personal ping-pong.

Construction
1. Cut the plywood to approximately 6" X 12". If the wood is too big to be held in the vice, refer to *Figure 14,* page 26.
2. Cut the handle from the 1 X 2 and fasten it underneath the table with two screws and some white glue. The 1 X 2 should stick out on one side about 4" (the handle) and about $1 1/2$" on the other side for a container to hold the ball.
3. From the stock of thin wood, cut one piece to run the full width of the table for the net. Fasten the net to the table with hot glue.
4. From the rest of the thin stock, cut three pieces (the net acts as the 4th side) and make a small box opposite the handle. Hot glue these pieces in place.
5. Paint the table green. After the paint dries, start practicing.

YAHOO STICK

The yahoo stick is a dowel with notches on the upper side and a propeller at one end *(Figure 110)*. As a second dowel is rubbed across the notches (in a certain way), a vibration pattern causes the propeller to spin. At the command of "yahoo, yahoo," the propeller reverses direction. Children enjoy the yahoo stick because it is so obviously not yelling "yahoo, yahoo" that makes the propeller reverse. Even when you know the secret, it takes some practice to perfect. The answer is revealed at the end of this section under **Using the Yahoo Stick**.

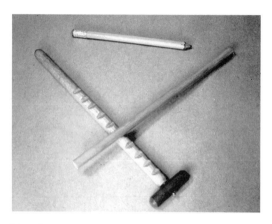

Figure 110.
The yahoo stick and the stick used to rub the notches. Learn to make the propeller reverse directions by yelling "yahoo, yahoo!"

Tools

- Sandpaper.
- Hammer.
- Eye protection.
- Drill with a bit slightly larger than the nail.
- Vice.
- Triangular file.
- Keyhole saw with hacksaw blade.

Materials

- Two 8" sections of $3/8$" dowel. Equivalent lengths of a branch would work, too.
- $1^1/2$" of $5/16$" dowel for the propeller.
- A $3/4$" nail with a head (not a finish nail) to attach the propeller.
- Oil or paint for finishing.

Construction

1. Cut two pieces of $3/8$" dowel 8" long. One will be for the yahoo stick itself and the other will be the stick that rubs the yahoo stick. Sand both *(Figure 111)*.
2. Use the corner of the triangular file to make 10 or 12 notches on one side of one of the 8" dowels. The notches should be about $1/8$" deep and $1/4$" apart.
3. Cut the propeller $1^1/4$" long from the $5/16$" dowel.
4. Drill a hole in the middle of the propeller. The hole should be slightly larger than the nail, so the propeller can spin freely. The hole should be in the exact middle of the propeller so it will be balanced. If one side of the propeller is heavier than the other, no

amount of vibration will cause it to spin. Find the approximate center by measuring or just by eyeballing. If you're a bit off, it doesn't matter because the next step tells how to compensate.

5. Balance the propeller. Place the nail through the propeller hole. Hold the nail horizontally so the propeller can turn freely. If the propeller is balanced, it will stay put, no matter where it is placed. If one end is heavier, the heavy end will always drop down. Sand the heavy end until the propeller balances.

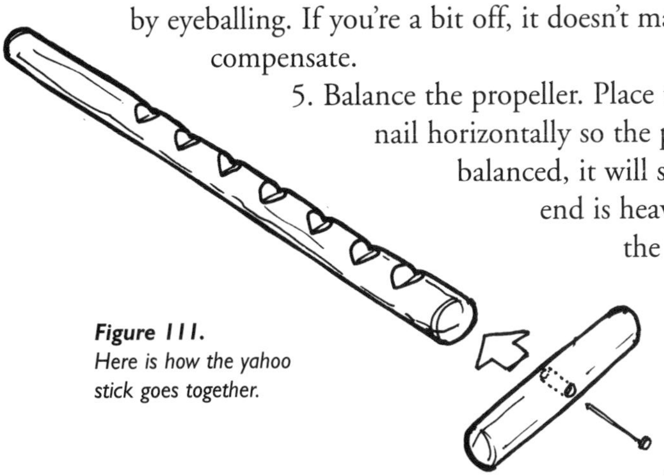

6. Fasten the propeller to the notched stick. Place the notched dowel in a vice with the propeller end up. Put the small nail through the balanced propeller and hold it over the notched dowel. Tap the nail in, but not too tightly. The propeller must be loose enough to spin on the nail.

Figure 111.
Here is how the yahoo stick goes together.

7. Painting or decoration. I suggest oiling the notched stick and dowel and painting the propeller. If the notched stick is painted, the paint will just be rubbed off by the dowel.

Using the Yahoo Stick

To spin the propeller, rub the notches on the yahoo stick back and forth with the dowel. At the same time, pull your finger back so it rubs, with some force, on the side of the yahoo stick *(Figure 112a)*. This should get the propeller turning clockwise. Sometimes your hands need to be adjusted, tighter or looser, further up or down one of the dowels, faster or slower. It may take some practice. I once had a teacher friend who wouldn't let me tell her how the yahoo stick worked and it took her two hours to figure it out herself.

To spin in the opposite direction, stop rubbing with the index finger and rub on the opposite side with your thumb *(Figure 112b)*. This will set up a different vibration pattern and cause the propeller to turn in the opposite direction. Unless someone is a very astute observer, she will miss this slight movement of your hand.

Figure 112a.

Figure 112b.

THE FLIPPER

The object of this toy is to use a plastic spoon to flip a small wooden ball into a film canister (*Figure 113*). This is a popular project. Although it looks simple to build, there are quite a few variables which must be just right or the flipper won't work.

Adult Preparation

A parent, teacher, or volunteer needs to assemble materials. You'll need fourteen inches of 1 X 2 and an inch of 2 X 2. These are standard sizes and shouldn't be hard to find. If 1 X 2 isn't available, or if you want to save wood and have access to a table saw, the base piece (1 X 2) can be cut thinner. Just set the saw for 1/2" and slice off sections from 2" material.

The block (the 2 X 2) could be smaller, too. Set the table saw for 1" and that can be cut from 2" material also.

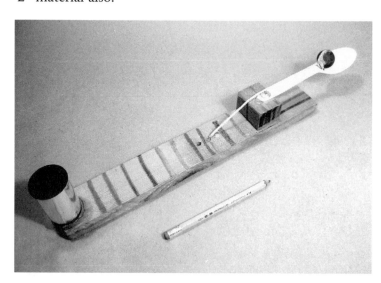

Figure 113.
The flipper. Use the spoon to flip the ball into the film canister.

Kids: Making the Flipper

Tools

- Saw.
- Low-temp hot glue gun and glue sticks.
- Vice.
- Drill bits.
- Candle or soldering iron for melting line so it won't unravel.
- Screwdriver plus brace and screwdriver bit for driving screws.
- Hand drill. Two drills are nice so you don't have to keep changing bits. One bit bigger than the smaller screw for drilling through the spoon. This should work for the string hole in the base and for pre-drilling the sheet rock screws, too. One smaller bit for pre-drilling the screw that holds the spoon.

Materials

- One plastic spoon per project. They break, so get extras.
- $1/2$" or $5/8$" wooden ball with a hole in the center. Or get the ball without the hole and let kids drill the hole themselves. Available in craft stores. A $5/8$" section from a dowel would work, too.
- $1/16$" nylon line, 2 feet per project.
- 1 X 2 about 14" long for the base piece. See "adult preparation" above.
- Block of wood $1^{1}/2$" X $1^{1}/2$" X 1". This is just a one-inch section from a 2 X 2.
- Film canister, available from just about any photo shop.
- One $3/4$" #6 screw, round head with a washer to match, for fastening the spoon to the block.
- Two $1^{1}/8$" sheetrock screws to fasten block to base.
- Markers or paint for decorating.

Construction

1. Cut base piece 14" long.
2. Fasten the spoon support block to the base. First, cut block to length (width of the base board) and drill pilot holes in the base. Pilot holes are a good idea in the support block *(Figure 114)*. Read the section on screws and pilot holes, pages 60-63. Be sure the top of the block is level, otherwise the spoon will throw the ball at an angle.
3. Fasten the spoon to the block. This involves drilling a hole in the spoon handle, drilling a smaller pilot hole in the spoon support block, and then putting a screw through the spoon into the support block. To drill a hole in the spoon handle, place the spoon in the vice so that just a small portion of the handle sticks up. Not too tight. Gently drill a hole through the handle with a bit just larger than the screw. The spoon will crack if too much pressure is applied. With the smaller bit, drill a pilot hole for the screw in the top of the block. Put the washer on the screw, put the screw through the hole in the spoon handle, and fasten the spoon to the block. After the screw is started, it may be easier to use the brace for the last few turns.

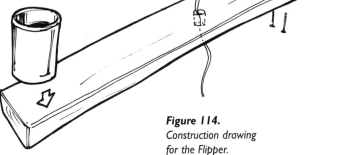

Figure 114.
Construction drawing for the Flipper.

4. Cut the string and tie it to the ball. If the string length is taken from the model, children often make it too short because they forget to add extra for the knots. Better too long than too short. Use two half hitches *(Figure 96*, page 116) and then put a little hot glue over the knot to make sure it won't unravel.

5. Figure out where to put the string hole in the base. This can be a bit confusing. Because a child's measurements will be a little, or maybe a lot, off, he can't copy placement of the string hole from the model. The hole needs to be very close to halfway between the spoon and the film canister. Measure and mark the halfway point (between spoon and canister) but don't drill it yet. Perform the following check first: temporarily glue, with just a tiny dab, a film canister at the end of the base piece. Put the ball in the spoon. Hold the string, without any slack, at the site of the hole. With the other hand, move the ball back and forth in an arc between the spoon and the canister. It should go from the center of the spoon to the center of the canister. If it doesn't, first try moving the canister. If that doesn't work, there may be some leeway in the ball's position in the spoon. Adjust that and see if it works. If the ball still doesn't go from spoon to canister then adjust the hole position. When you think your mark is in the right position, drill the hole. Thread the string through it, squirt a tiny bit of hot glue in the hole to temporarily hold it, and test again. If it works, reinforce the canister and the string with more hot glue, and you're set. If it doesn't work, either drill another hole in the appropriate direction or move the canister and try again.

6. Once the flipper is working, the final step is to decorate. Markers, paint, different colors of shelf paper or some combination of all three are popular.

MARBLE ROLL

A few years back I was teaching preschool carpentry and a friend lent me a small wooden marble roll to use in class. It consisted of two upright 1 X 4s connected by sloping, grooved troughs. The marbles rolled down the troughs, reversing direction in a zigzag fashion, to the bottom. The kids would roll one marble down by itself, then two or three, then a whole handful. Over and over and over again. This inspired me to design a marble roll kids could build themselves and take home. It consists of a cardboard back approximately 18" square to which are glued paths and obstacles for the marble to encounter *(Figure 115)*. It is one of the favorite projects of older children.

Figure 115.
Jason with the marble roll he constructed.

Adult Preparation

A parent, teacher, or volunteer cuts cardboard and beveled strips. Cut the beveled strips like the bottom drawing in *Figure 41*, page 55.

- A refrigerator carton, available at appliance stores, will make 15 or 20 marble roll back-pieces. If you just have one or two kids, a large cardboard box will do. I use a mat knife to cut the cardboard ahead of time but kids could cut their own cardboard using a small saw. I don't allow kids to use mat knives.
- Cut 1/8" X 3/4" strips with a beveled edge for the paths that the marbles will follow. The bevel will slant the strip toward the cardboard and keep the marble from rolling off the front. To do this I set my table saw at a slight bevel and make lots of strips at one time.

Kids: Making the Marble Roll

Tools

- Keyhole saw.
- Eye protection.
- Low-temperature hot glue gun and glue sticks.
- Wire cutters. These work great for cutting popsicle or stir sticks. It isn't necessary to cut all the way through the wood. Just crimp it and then bend back and forth till it breaks.

- Vice.
- Screwdriver and brace with screwdriver bit.

Materials

For the stand you'll need:
- A piece of cardboard approximately 18" square for each project.
- 1 X 6 about 8" long. This will be cut at an angle and screwed to the back of the cardboard to keep it upright.
- Two $1^{3}/_{8}$" sheetrock screws for fastening the cardboard to the wood stand.

For the marble roll itself you will need:
- Lots of $^{3}/_{4}$" wide X $^{1}/_{8}$" thick wood strips cut with a bevel.
- Coffee stir sticks, popsicle or craft sticks for miscellaneous attachments.
- Miscellaneous small scrap wood.
- Film canisters. Students can cut these down to form tunnels or small cups to catch the marble. The easiest way to cut a film canister is to slide the open end over a big dowel or broom handle that is held in a vice and cut the canister with a fine tooth keyhole saw.
- Decorations: markers, paint, and aluminum foil.
- Miscellaneous gears, screws etc. from taking apart VCRs.

Construction

- Make a stand (a piece of 1 X 6 cut lengthwise at an angle) for the cardboard. Sometimes I'll cut these pieces at home on the band saw and fasten them to the cardboard before class, so kids can have more time for the actual marble roll construction.
- Using the two sheetrock screws, fasten the stand to the cardboard so it will hold the cardboard at an angle *(Figure 116)*. Hold the stand where you want it to end up. Draw around it. Poke holes (smaller than the screws) in the cardboard inside the outline. Hold the stand and cardboard together again and put the screws in. After the screws are started it may be easier for kids to put the stand in the vice and use the brace to drive the screws.

Before the construction of the actual marble roll begins, I tell kids:

1. "The beveled strips need to slope towards the cardboard (not away from it) to keep the marbles on track." This is obvious when you see it, but easy to miss.

2. "Fasten one piece at a time and test with a marble before gluing." Tacking with a tiny amount of glue and then testing is one way to do it. Sometimes kids will glue several pieces to the cardboard without testing and are surprised when the marble doesn't follow the path they anticipate. Glue and test.

3. "Gentle slopes and short runs are best. Too much slope, and the run will be over before it starts."

4. "It isn't necessary to run glue over the whole length of a strip. Long runs of glue often dry before they fasten anything. Three drops of glue is enough to hold the longest strips."

Kids will come up with the most interesting and creative marble rolls, going through amazing engineering contortions to keep the marble on track. The teacher's role is to help problem-solve.

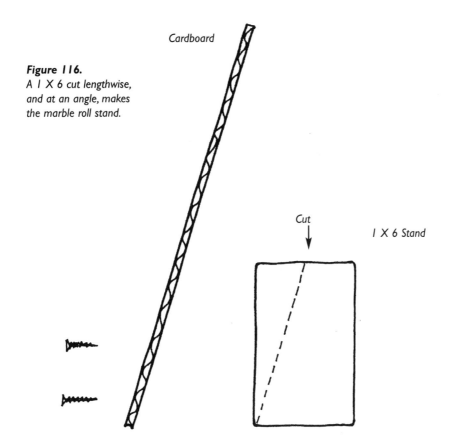

Cardboard

Figure 116.
*A 1 X 6 cut lengthwise,
and at an angle, makes
the marble roll stand.*

Cut

1 X 6 Stand

THE PEGGED BOX

After kids have made the basic box, they may want to try a box held together with pegs instead of glue *(Figure 117)*. For this box, in addition to the materials for the basic box (page 119), you will need:

Figure 117.
This box will stay together without glue but a little glue makes it a lot stronger.

Tools
• A drill with a $1/8$" bit.

Materials
• Strips of wood, $5/8$" or $3/4$" X $11/2$", for two of the box sides.
• Strips of wood, $1/4$" X $11/2$", for the other box sides.
• A $1/8$" dowel.
• Some thick rubber bands.
• White glue.
• A toothpick for putting glue in the peg holes.

Construction
1. Cut the sides the same as for the basic box, only make two from the thicker material. Thicker pieces will make it easier to drill holes for the pegs.
2. Once the sides are cut, assemble the four sides of the box and hold them together with thick rubber bands. The thin wood should lap over the top of the thick wood.

3. Cut twelve 1" pegs from the 1/8" dowel with the keyhole saw.

4. Fasten the box together with pegs. Place the box in the vice so the sides are being clamped together *(Figure 118)*. The box should be buried in the vice except for the corner that's going to be drilled. Hold the drill horizontally. Drill one hole. Put a bit of

Figure 118.
*The box held in the vice
ready for the first hole to
be drilled.*

white glue in the hole with a toothpick and tap in a peg. Let it stick out for now; it can be cut and/or sanded down later. Check the alignment of the corner joint and drill another hole. Put in the second peg. Two pegs per corner should do it for a small box. Work around the box one corner at a time. Check alignment each time before drilling. After the box is pegged together and the glue dries, cut and sand the pegs so they are flush with the outside of the box.

5. Measure and cut pieces for the bottom just as you did with the basic box. Fasten with pegs in the same manner as the sides were fastened. Make a lid and fasten it with a leather hinge, as with the basic box, if desired.

BRANCH BOX

My son Andrew built this birch box *(Figures 119 and 120)* for his mom when he was in the 6th grade. These can be very beautiful if the top is sanded carefully. The hardest part of this project is cutting out the inside of the box with a coping saw. If I suspect the child might have difficulty with the coping saw, I might suggest he build the puzzle project first (page 78) to test how he likes using the coping saw.

Figure 119.
The branch box.

Figure 120.

Tools

- Handsaw.
- Coping saw.
- Square piece of wood 1" X 1".
- Low-temperature hot glue gun and glue sticks.
- Vice.
- Drill with 1/4" bit.
- Eye protection.

Materials

- A section of a branch 2"- 4" in diameter. Woods that are easy to cut are the best. I use mostly cedar and birch. Oak or maple would certainly look nice, but would be considerably harder to cut.
- 1/8" plywood for the box bottom. Wood that isn't plywood would be OK too, if it's not too thick.
- Leather for the bottom of the box, both inside and out, if desired.
- Mineral oil for finishing the box top.
- Sandpaper for sanding box top: 80 and 220 grit.

Construction

The pieces of the box should be assembled in the order they are cut. To avoid confusion, as each piece is cut, mark how it mates up with the piece it is cut from. For example, after the lid has been cut mark a "1" on the underside of the lid, and a matching "1" on the top of the box body so you know these pieces fit together by matching the "ones". Mark every piece in a similar manner, but with different numbers.

1. Choose a branch 2"- 4" in diameter. The smaller diameter box, the less coping saw cutting involved. Also, the taller the box, the more difficult to cut. 2" is about maximum height before cutting becomes unmanageable.

2. Cut the lid first. Put the branch in the vice and slice a $1/2$" section from one end. Try to make this cut a uniform thickness. Mark matching surfaces.

3. The top of the lid can be sanded and oiled anytime. It's not a bad idea to save this work for a break from cutting the center section out.

4. Make the box body by moving down the branch 1"- $1^{1}/2$", depending on how tall the box is to be, and make a second cut.

5. Cut the center section of the branch out with the coping saw. If you haven't already done so, read the section on coping saws (pages 29-30).
   • Draw a line for the coping saw to follow, parallel to and about $3/8$" in from the outside of the branch. This should result in a rough circle $3/8$" smaller than the branch.
   • Drill a $5/16$" hole just inside this line.
   • Remove the blade from the coping saw, place it through the hole and reattach it to the saw. Place the branch in the vice and cut out the inside of the box.

6. Mark the top of the center piece (the piece just removed) and save it for the next step.

7. To keep the lid from sliding around, cut the stopper piece ($1/4$" slice) from the top of the piece removed from the center of the box. You can see this stopper piece on the underside of the lid in *Figure 120*. The trick is to put it in the right place on the bottom of the lid. To do this, put the lid on the box, carefully checking alignment, and turn the box upside down. Reach through the bottom of the box with a sharp pencil and mark the joint where the lid meets the box. The stopper piece will go inside this pencil line. Remove the lid, and glue the stopper in place.

8. Make the bottom of the box. Place the box on the $1/8$" plywood and draw around it. Cut the bottom out and glue it on to the box (hot glue is OK).

9. Cut leather for the box bottom, both inside and the outside, and glue it in place.

GLOCKENSPIEL

The glockenspiel *(Figure 121)* is similar to a xylophone but made from pipe instead of flat metal bars. Different lengths of pipe will give different notes. If care is taken to keep the pipe measurements accurate, the glockenspiel will be sort of tuned.

Tools
- Handsaw.
- Tape measure.
- Vice.
- Fine round file.
- Sandpaper.
- Eye protection.
- Nail set to sink finish nails.
- Plumbing pipe cutter. Available at hardware stores.

- Hammer.
- Square.

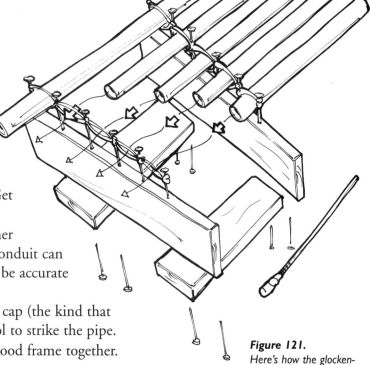

Materials
- 42" of 1 X 2.
- Twelve 1½" nails with heads.
- Six 2" medium rubber bands. Get extras. They break.
- 60" of ½" plumbing pipe. Other diameters of pipe or electrical conduit can be used, but pipe lengths won't be accurate for notes.
- 8" long small dowel and rubber cap (the kind that goes on a chair foot) for the tool to strike the pipe.
- Eight 1½" nails to fasten the wood frame together.

Figure 121.
Here's how the glockenspiel goes together.

Construction
1. Cut 1 X 2s to length: two 14", one 6" and one 8" long. Sand.
2. Assemble wood pieces. I think it's is a good idea to drill pilot holes for the nails holding the four wood pieces together. Set all the boards in position marking where they will fit together. Then mark the position of the nail holes. Take it apart, drill the holes, reassemble, and nail together.
3. Lay out the position for the nails, about 1¾" apart, on the top edge of the 1 X 2s *(Figure 121)*.

4. Pound the nails (1^1/2") in at the marked positions. The nails should go in about ^{1}/2". A block under the 1 X 2s, to keep them from bouncing as the nails are being pounded, will make the nails go in easier.

5. Cut the pipe to the following lengths using a pipe cutter: 13^9/16", 12^7/8", 11^3/16", 11^1/16", 10^1/2". *Figure 123* shows a pipe cutter. To cut pipe, mark where the pipe is to be

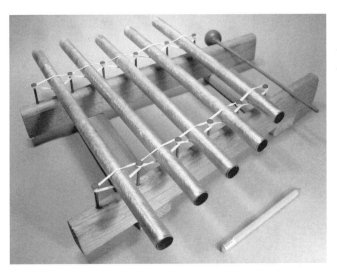

Figure 122.
The glockenspiel is constructed from plumbing pipe and 1 X 2's.

cut, and put the pipe in the vice so it's sticking straight up. Pipe cutters have a cutting wheel and two rollers. Open the cutter up (that is, increase the distance between the rollers and the cutting wheel) and slip it over the pipe so that the cutting wheel is on top of the mark. Tighten the rollers down tight against the pipe. Spin the cutter around the pipe once or twice, and then tighten the rollers another half turn, pushing the pipe into the cutting wheel. That's how it works: cut around the pipe, push the pipe deeper into the cutting wheel, again and again, until the pipe is in two pieces.

6. File and/or sand inside the pipe ends to remove sharp edges. The holes at the ends of the pipes seem to attract little fingers, so check each hole carefully.

7. Stretch rubber bands between 3 or 4 nails, two per side. Wrap each side of the rubber band around each nail.

8. Install pipe between the rubber bands.

9. Cut dowel mallet, fit cap, and test. The glockenspiel can be tuned by cutting the pipe pieces a little long and then trimming them ^{1}/8" at a time until they correspond to the proper note on a piano.

Figure 123.
The pipe cutter ready to cut pipe.

DO-NOTHING-MACHINE

The do-nothing-machine *(Figure 124)* is an old folk toy. It consists of a 3¹/2" square block with dovetail grooves crossing in the center of the block. Two small wedge-shaped blocks fit into grooves and are attached to a handle. As the handle turns, the wedges slide back and forth in the grooves, never meeting. Usually I save this project for third graders or older, who have built a few other projects.

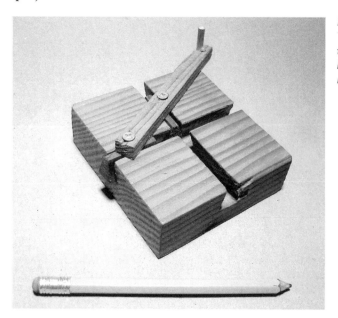

Figure 124.
The do-nothing-machine is the perfect thing to give kids when they say, "there's nothing to do."

Some wiseacre asked me if there was anything the do-nothing-machine could do. The kids came up with two things. The first was to sort peas. If peas were slowly dropped in the exact center of the do-nothing-machine as the handle turned, peas would be divided into four different piles. Someone else suggested the do-nothing-machine could draw an ellipse. Put the do-nothing-machine in the center of a piece of paper and hold a pencil straight up and down at the end of the handle so the point is resting on the paper. Follow the handle as it makes one rotation. The resulting shape will be an ellipse.

Adult Preparation

A parent, teacher, or volunteer needs to cut the dovetails in the do-nothing-machine, cut the wedges that slide in the dovetail grooves, and cut pieces for the handle.

Tools for Preparation
- Vice.
- Handsaw.
- Router with dovetail bit.
- Table saw for cutting blocks, handle strips, and dovetail wedges.
- Jig for cutting dovetails.
- Eye protection.

Materials
- A piece of plywood about 8" X 12" for the base of the jig.
- About 36" of 1 X 4 for the jig.
- Six 1¹/8" sheetrock screws.

Construction
1. Cut dovetails into 3¹/2" X 3¹/2" X ³/4" blocks. First, set up a guide so the router bit will run the the length of an eight foot 1 X 4 thus cutting the lengthwise dovetail for approximately 25 machines in one pass. Next, set up a jig to hold the 1 X 4 and guide the router for the second dovetail. *Figure 125* shows the jig. Lastly, cut the 1 X 4 into 3¹/2" blocks. Kids could cut their own blocks from the long strip.
2. Cut wedge strips slightly bigger than the dovetails. They could be cut to fit, but I didn't want to make this project too easy.
3. Cut ³/8" X ¹/2" X 4" strips for the handle.

Figure 125.
A jig for cutting the second dovetail in the blocks.

Kids: Building the Do-Nothing-Machine

Tools
- Vice.
- Eye protection.
- Screwdriver to match screws.
- A keyhole saw with a hacksaw blade.
- Sandpaper (6" X 6") fastened to boards screwed down to the workbench.
- Small pieces of sandpaper hot glued to the end of popsicle sticks.
- A drill. If you are working with one or two children, one drill is sufficient. You'll just

have to change bits. If you are working with a group of kids, two drills are nice and three are better yet. There are three sizes of holes to drill so if each drill has a different bit, there will be less confusion and less bit changing.
- Three drill bits: one to drill a pilot hole for the screw, one a hair larger than the screw shank, and one $1/8$" bit to drill for the dowel handle.
- Low-temperature hot glue gun and glue sticks.

Materials

- $3^{1}/2$" X $3^{1}/2$" X 1" block with intersecting dovetail grooves cut into the block. I use pine because it doesn't splinter as much as fir or cedar. I'm sure other woods will work.
- $1/2$" X $1/4$" X 4" piece, one for the handle of each machine.
- $1/2$" section of $1/8$" dowel for a peg at the end of the handle.
- Two $3/4$" #6 wood screws to hold the handle to the dovetail pieces.
- A 2" length of wood the same shape as the dovetail only slightly larger. This will be cut into two pieces.
- Mineral oil or petroleum jelly to lubricate the wedges and slots. A small paint brush for the mineral oil.

Construction

1. Use the popsicle sticks with sandpaper glued on them to sand the dovetail slots in the blocks. The dovetail grooves will be rough from the router cut. Sand off all the little slivers, especially at the intersecting grooves.
2. Cut the wedges 1" long and sand to fit dovetail slots. Measurements should be taken from a working model. Sand the wedges until they will slide easily down the dovetail slot. Sand the wedge by moving it lengthwise over the sandpaper. Sanding the wedge sideways often results in a rounded wedge, too narrow at the top, and too wide at the bottom.
3. Cut and sand the handle.
4. Copy the positions for the holes in the handle and wedges from the model.
5. Drill the five holes. The largest hole ($1/8$") is for the dowel handle peg. Two medium holes go through the handle. They need to be bigger than the screw shank so the screws will rotate as the handle turns. The smallest holes are in the wedges.
   • Drill the small holes (appropriate size for the screw) in the top center of the wedges. I use a nail for a bit instead of a drill bit because kids will break the smaller drill bits. Put the wedge in a vice, but be careful not to tighten the vice too much or the wedge will be crushed.
   • Drill the $1/8$" hole in the end of the handle for the dowel-peg. This requires a light touch as it is easy to split the handle by pressing down too hard.
   • To mark the position of the medium sized holes (in the handle), first set the wedges in adjacent slots halfway between the edge and the center of the do-nothing-machine. Hold

the handle over the top of the wedges, as if it were assembled. Pretending to look through the handle, mark the handle directly above the wedge holes. After the hole locations are marked, drill two holes with the medium sized bit.

6. Assemble. Cut and glue the short dowel peg into the larger hole at the end of the handle. Set the wedges in adjacent slots halfway between the edge and center. Put the handle on top of the wedges, aligning the holes in the handle with the holes in the wedges. Put screws through the handle into the wedges and tighten the screws, but not too tight. The handle must be able to pivot on the wedge.

7. To help the wedges slide, put a liberal amount of mineral oil or petroleum jelly in the dovetail slots and on the wedges *(Figure 126)*.

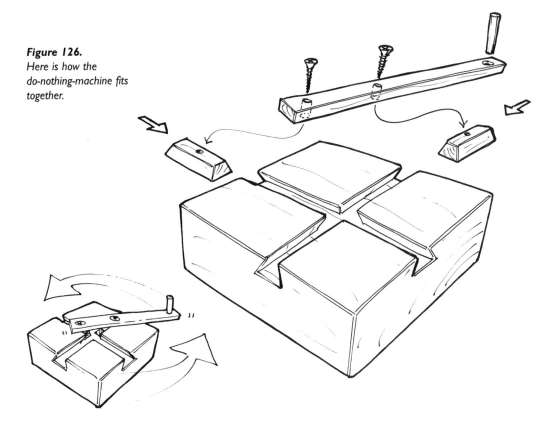

Figure 126.
Here is how the do-nothing-machine fits together.

Troubleshooting

Seldom does a do-nothing-machine work perfectly from the beginning. Most have to be gently broken in. Make sure the screws aren't too tight, a common mistake. Rather than holding the handle by the peg, hold it more in the center of the handle and turn slowly. Turn the handle until it stops and then try reversing direction. All do-nothing-machines get looser with use. Often a do-nothing-machine which barely turns at first is zipping around, doing nothing, after a few minutes of cranking.

STEP STOOL

Although kids liked the camping stool project, some wanted a more stable platform so they could help in the kitchen or workshop or just have a kid-sized place to sit *(Figure 127)*.

Figure 127.
The step stool is a handy piece of furniture.

Tools
- Vice.
- Eye protection.
- Square.
- Screwdriver to match sheetrock screws.
- Countersink.
- Handsaw.
- Brace and bit to match screws.
- Tape measure.

Materials
- 34" of 1 X 10 pine. 1 X 8 would also work. ³/₄" plywood could be used, too.
- Eight 1⁵/₈" sheetrock screws.

Construction *(Figure 128)*
1. Cut out the seat. Square cuts are especially important for the legs and the cross brace, so cutting the seat first will give extra practice cutting straight. The seat should be 10" long and square on both ends. Some students may want to use a coping saw to round the corners to give their stool a more finished appearance.
2. Cut two legs 8" long. Both ends of each leg must be square. The remaining wood is the brace.
3. Drill the holes for the screws which fasten the legs to the brace. To locate the position for these holes, draw a light pencil line on the centerline (up and down) of the leg. Drill two holes on this line, one 1¹/₄" from the top, and the other 3" down. Countersink on the outside to recess the screw heads. Do this for both legs.

4. Lay out the upside-down V at the bottom of the leg. Measure $2^{1}/2$" up from the bottom of the leg on the centerline and put a small mark. At the very bottom of the stool, measure 1" from the centerline to both the right and the left, and mark both positions. Connect the marks to form an upside-down V and cut out.

5. Round corners (if desired) and sand everything.

6. Lay out the position of the legs on the bottom of the seat (use a square) by drawing two parallel lines between which each leg will fit. The first line should be $1^{1}/2$" in from the end and the second line should be $3/4$" beyond the first line.

7. Mark places for two screws, equally spaced, between these parallel lines.

8. Drill holes at the marked positions. Flip the seat over to the top and use a countersink (or large drill bit) to indent the wood a bit so the screws will sit below the surface of the wood.

9. Fasten the seat to the legs. Sink the screws down through the top of the seat until they barely poke out the other side. Set the leg vertically in the vice and hold the seat over it in position. You will have to get down on the floor and look up to do this. The screw points, which should be sticking out, will keep the two pieces aligned while you drive the screws in. This operation is a two-person job and I'll usually help align, and then hold, the first leg as the screws are being driven. Children can help each other with the second leg.

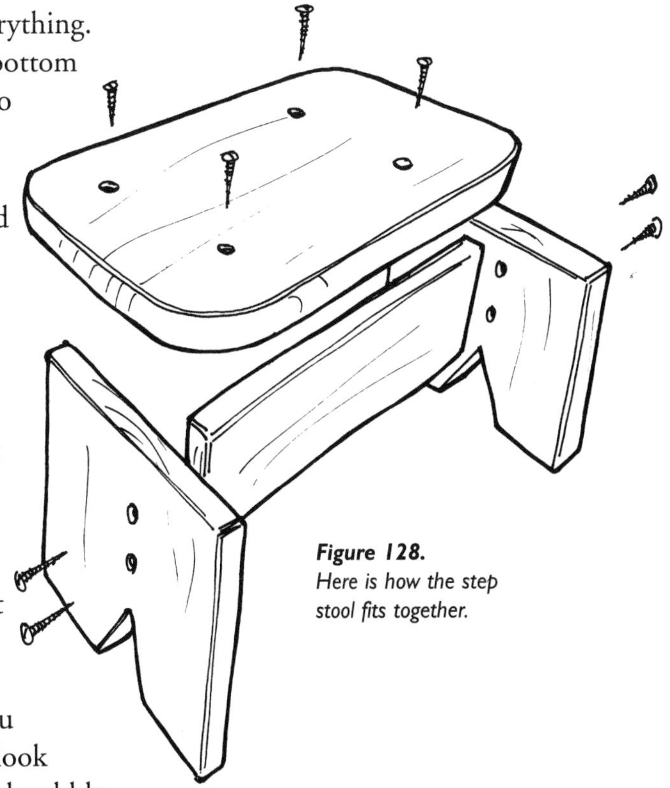

Figure 128.
Here is how the step stool fits together.

10. Cut the brace and fasten it in. Use a tape to measure the actual distance between the top of the two legs because it won't be the $5^{1}/2$" it theoretically should be. Cut the brace to this measured length. Start screws in both legs till they poke out just a hair. Slide the brace in place and finish driving the screws.

Troubleshooting

The inability to cut straight is the most frequently encountered problem. The trick to cutting straight is to not let the saw get far from the line in the first place. Watch the junction where the saw teeth meet the line. If the saw wanders, even the slightest bit, twist the saw handle gently back toward the line. Once a cut is $1/8$" off, there is not much to be done but don't throw the board away. Draw another square line, making the board $3/8$" shorter, and try again.

WHIRLPOOL BOTTLES

You can buy a small bottle-connector fitting to make this project, but I like to make them myself. **Safety Note:** This project requires close adult supervision because an electric hot glue gun must be used in the vicinity of a bottle filled with water. For a safe setup:

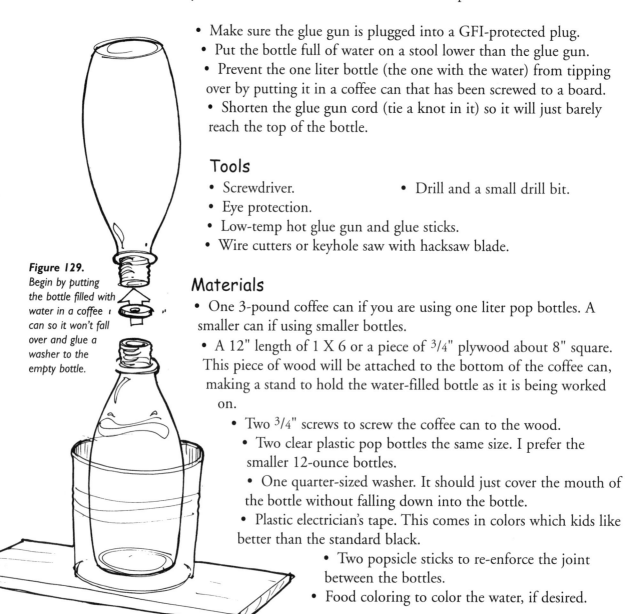

Figure 129.
Begin by putting the bottle filled with water in a coffee can so it won't fall over and glue a washer to the empty bottle.

- Make sure the glue gun is plugged into a GFI-protected plug.
- Put the bottle full of water on a stool lower than the glue gun.
- Prevent the one liter bottle (the one with the water) from tipping over by putting it in a coffee can that has been screwed to a board.
- Shorten the glue gun cord (tie a knot in it) so it will just barely reach the top of the bottle.

Tools

- Screwdriver.
- Eye protection.
- Low-temp hot glue gun and glue sticks.
- Wire cutters or keyhole saw with hacksaw blade.
- Drill and a small drill bit.

Materials

- One 3-pound coffee can if you are using one liter pop bottles. A smaller can if using smaller bottles.
- A 12" length of 1 X 6 or a piece of 3/4" plywood about 8" square. This piece of wood will be attached to the bottom of the coffee can, making a stand to hold the water-filled bottle as it is being worked on.
- Two 3/4" screws to screw the coffee can to the wood.
- Two clear plastic pop bottles the same size. I prefer the smaller 12-ounce bottles.
- One quarter-sized washer. It should just cover the mouth of the bottle without falling down into the bottle.
- Plastic electrician's tape. This comes in colors which kids like better than the standard black.
- Two popsicle sticks to re-enforce the joint between the bottles.
- Food coloring to color the water, if desired.

Construction

1. Drill two holes in the bottom of the coffee can and then screw through the can into the board. Set this apparatus on a stool lower than the glue gun.
2. Fill one bottle 3/4 full of water and set it in the coffee can/board apparatus. Add food coloring if desired.
3. Glue the washer over the mouth of the other bottle *(Figure 129)*.
4. Hot glue the two bottles together. Put glue all the way around the joint. While the glue is still warm, wrap several layers of colored electrician's tape tightly around the joint between the two bottles *(Figure 130)*. Now the joint should be waterproof, but it isn't very strong.
5. Reinforce the joint between the bottles. Cut four popsicle sticks in half (maybe a little smaller) to make splints and hot glue them over the top of the colored tape. Wrap several more layers of colored tape over the top of these sticks. This should make a joint that is both waterproof and strong *(Figure 131)*.

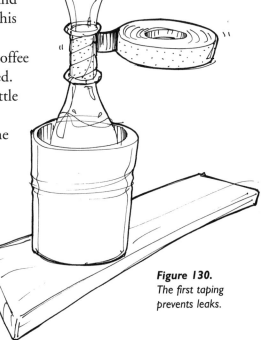

Figure 130.
The first taping prevents leaks.

Using the Whirlpool Bottles

The Whirlpool Bottles are actually a science experiment about air and water. Turn the bottles over so the water is in the top bottle. Keep holding the bottles so they won't fall over. What happens? A little water spills into the bottom bottle but most of it stays in the top bottle. Why is this? Although the bottom bottle looks empty, it is actually full of air. To get water to the bottom bottle, the air must go to the top bottle. If the bottles are shaken up and down you'll see some air go up (bubbles) and some water go down, but an equilibrium is reached, and most of the water stays in the top bottle.

Figure 131.
The second taping strengthens the joint.

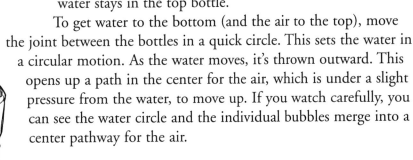

To get water to the bottom (and the air to the top), move the joint between the bottles in a quick circle. This sets the water in a circular motion. As the water moves, it's thrown outward. This opens up a path in the center for the air, which is under a slight pressure from the water, to move up. If you watch carefully, you can see the water circle and the individual bubbles merge into a center pathway for the air.

THUMB PIANO

Tools

- Handsaw.
- Wire cutters.
- Vice.
- Sandpaper.
- Keyhole saw with hacksaw blade.
- A drill bit for the sheetrock screw pilot holes.
- A bit bigger than the screws for drilling through the aluminum strip.

- A countersink.
- Hammer.
- Eye protection.
- Hand drill.

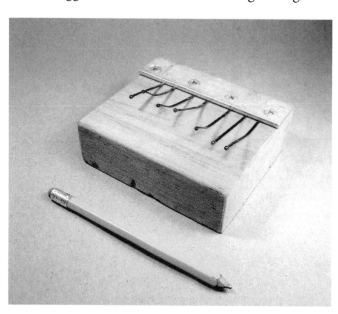

Figure 132.
Thumb piano.

Materials

- A block of wood approximately 4" X 3¹/2" X 1¹/2" thick. A 4" chunk from a 2 X 4 may work, but harder wood, like maple or oak, is better because the screws can be put in tighter without stripping the threads out.
- Four large bobby pins for the piano keys.
- An aluminum bar (available at hardware stores) 4" long by 1" wide by ¹/8" thick to hold the bobby pins down. Steel or brass would work, too, but would be harder to drill. Wood might be worth a try if you don't have a strip of aluminum handy.
- Four 1³/8" screws to hold the aluminum strip down.
- Oil or paint as desired *(Figure 132)*.

Construction

1. Cut the block of wood 4" long.
2. Using the hacksaw, cut the aluminum bar to the same length as the block.
3. Drill four equally spaced holes in the aluminum bar. Countersink the holes so the screws will be flush with the top of the bar.
4. Drill pilot holes in the wood block to match each hole position on the metal bar. To mark the position of these holes, set the metal bar on top of the wood block and mark through the holes.
5. The following is an adult job. Wear eye protection. Use the wire cutters to cut the bobby pins to the following lengths: 2", $2^{1}/8$", $2^{1}/4$", $2^{3}/8$", $2^{1}/2$", $2^{5}/8$", and $2^{3}/4$" *(Figure 133).*

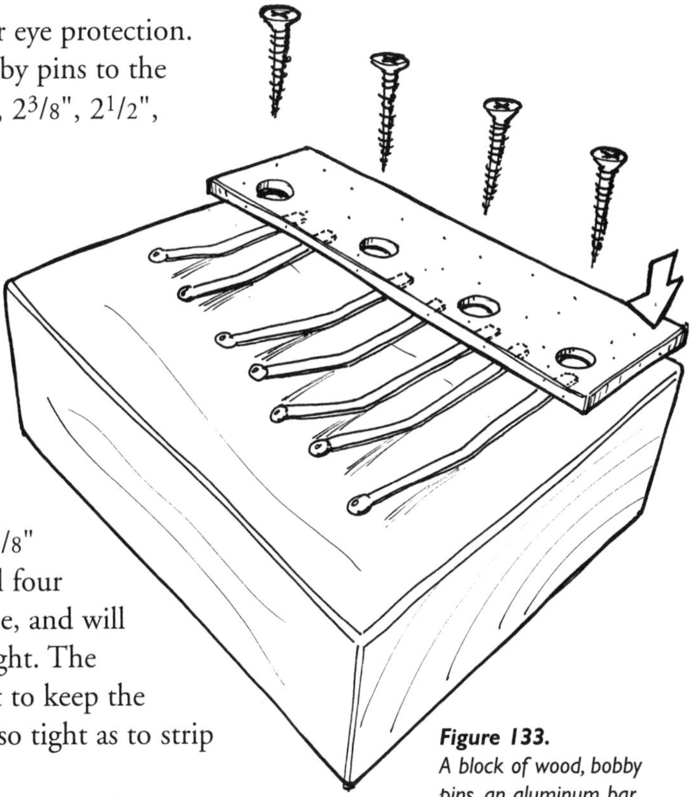

Assembly

1. Flatten the ends of the bobby pins (so they will fit under the bar) by pounding them with the hammer on a hard flat surface.
2. Start all four screws and tighten until there is just barely enough room under the bar for the bobby pins. Place each bobby pin about $^{3}/8$" under the metal bar and tighten all four screws. This is easier said than done, and will take some fooling around to get right. The screws need to be brought up tight to keep the bobby pins from moving, but not so tight as to strip out the wood threads.
3. Bend the keys (bobby pins) up a bit so they have room to vibrate.
4. Oil or paint to suit.

Figure 133.
A block of wood, bobby pins, an aluminum bar, and screws are all that are needed to make a thumb piano.

Troubleshooting

If the bar won't keep the bobby pins tight, the screws have probably been put in too tight, stripping out the threads inside the wood. Try fatter screws. Another alternative would be to replace the screws with $^{3}/16$" X $1^{3}/4$" flat head machine screws and nuts. If you choose this option, countersink the screw heads (on the bottom of the block) so they won't stick out and mar the surface holding the thumb piano.

WHEELED VEHICLES
Wheels

The hardest part of making vehicles *(Figure 134)* is making wheels. You can buy wheels at various craft or hardware/home improvement centers. The smaller wheels aren't too expensive. If you only have a few kids, this isn't a bad option. But if you have a lot of kids or want bigger wheels, it gets a bit pricey. Besides, why buy wheels when kids can make them? Here are some options:

Figure 134.
The car Amanda built when she was in kinder-garten.

Wheels that don't turn can be made by cutting 1/4" to 1/2" thick sections from dowels or by using the lids from film canisters. Kids use these a lot on airplanes and as steering wheels for boats or cars. Wheels that turn are more popular, but require more work.

The easiest turning wheel can be made from the plastic (some are cardboard) center tube of fax paper rolls *(Figure 135)*. These work well for smaller wheels and steering wheels, too. Using a keyhole saw with a hacksaw blade, cut a 1/4" section off the tube. Use an appropriate sized dowel for the axle. Glue a short slightly bigger dowel on the end of the axle as a hubcap to keep the wheel from sliding off.

Here is what you need to make wheels that turn from dowels:

Tools

- A center finder.
- Vice.
- Hammer.
- Eye protection.
- A nail to mark the position to start the drill.
- Keyhole saw with hacksaw blade.
- Handsaw.
- Sandpaper.
- Drill and 1/4" bit.

Materials

- Dowels of different diameters for wheels.

Figure 135.
Wheels made from the plastic center tube of fax paper rolls.

Construction

1. Cut a thin section off the end of a dowel for the wheel itself. The miter block (page 187) will help make these cuts uniform so the wheels come out the same thickness.
2. Locate the center of the wheel with the center finder (page 74). This is where the axle should go, so drill a hole here.
3. Make an indentation here with a nail to start the hole and keep the bit from wandering away from center.
4. After the correct size hole is drilled, all you need is some sort of hubcap to keep the wheel from falling off. A dowel slightly larger than the axle is one option. I've also used short pieces of popsicle sticks as hubcaps.
5. To make the actual car is straightforward. All you need are miscellaneous pieces of wood and imagination.

KALEIDOSCOPE

My niece gave me an unusually simple kaleidoscope for Christmas. It was made from three one-inch-wide mirrors, facing inward, fastened together in a triangular tube. It was open at both ends. The mirror surfaces reflected and re-reflected the image of anything placed close to one end. I had some plastic mirror in the basement so I wondered if.......

Adult Preparation

A parent, teacher, or volunteer needs to make a jig to hold the plastic strips together as they are being glued.

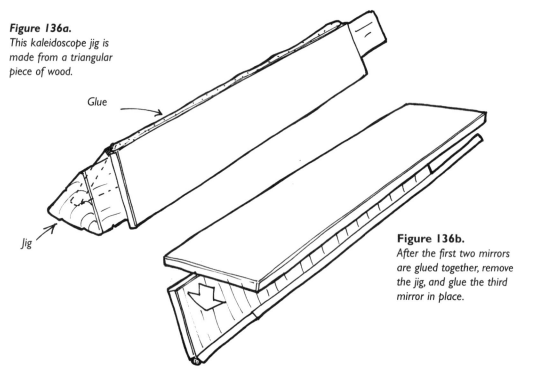

Figure 136a.
This kaleidoscope jig is made from a triangular piece of wood.

Glue

Jig

Figure 136b.
After the first two mirrors are glued together, remove the jig, and glue the third mirror in place.

The difficult part of building the kaleidoscope is holding the first two strips of plastic together, in some semblance of a triangle, while the glue dries. To make this task easier for kids, I cut a triangular piece of wood about 6" long to act as a jig. In cross section, this jig is an equilateral triangle, with 60 degree corners. Each face should be about 1" wide. You will need a piece of wood at least an inch thick. A table saw will make quick work of this job, but it could be made by hand, too. After the triangle piece is cut, use the Surform plane to round the peaks off the triangle. Rounding the corners will make it less likely to glue the jig to the plastic strips. Or maybe a jig could be made from modeling clay.

Kids: Building the Kaleidoscope

Tools

- Vice.
- Sandpaper.
- Keyhole saw with a hacksaw blade.
- Rubber bands.
- Eye protection.
- Low-temp hot glue gun and glue sticks.

Materials

- Plastic mirror. Small pieces (1" X 6") are often available from places that sell glass. Ask for free scraps.
- Red, blue, yellow, green, and orange electrician's tape.

Construction

1. Cut three pieces of plastic mirror 1" X 6". The plastic mirror is brittle, so use the keyhole saw with a hacksaw blade. Hold the mirror in the vice close to the cut. After the pieces are cut, sand the cuts to smooth up the edges.
2. Hold two of the mirrored pieces on the triangle jig so their edges meet and the mirrors face in. This is tricky. If it is helpful, use rubber bands to help hold the mirrors in place. Glue these two pieces in place with just a few drops of hot glue. Be careful not to glue the plastic to the jig. Wait until the glue dries. Remove the jig *(Figure 136a)*.
3. Glue the third plastic strip in place with just a few drops, too. The jig won't be necessary for this last piece *(Figure 136b)*. If the triangle shape seems fairly uniform then go back and reinforce the glue joints.
4. After the glue has dried, cover the outside of the kaleidoscope with colored tape and it's finished.

"LOG" CABIN

I thought a mini house might be an interesting project so I cut up a bunch of $3/4$" X $3/4$" strips and tried to talk someone into building the first one. No one seemed interested, so I had to build the model myself. It was pretty humdrum and sat on the shelf, never drawing comments or interest *(Figure 137)*. One day I said, "Tomorrow's project of the day is log houses." No one seemed to object and I even detected a bit of interest. The kids had a good time and we ended up with a very interesting array of houses. Mine was far and away the most boring. Its only redeeming design feature was the hinged roof, which some kids copied. Since then I've done the "house project" several times and the only change I made was to switch to wider "logs" to make the project move a bit faster.

Figure 137.
My not-so-imaginative house. The only thing I liked was the hinged roof which several kids copied.

Adult Preparation:

A parent, teacher, or volunteer needs to cut the "log" strips. This project hinges on having a table saw to cut strips lengthwise from 2 X 4s for the logs. Set the saw to about $3/16$". Cut lots of strips, 20 or 25 feet per child for each house. You can always find a use for the extra strips.

Kids: Building the "Log" Cabin

Tools

- Handsaw.
- Miter block (page 187).
- Low-temp hot glue gun and glue sticks.
- Vice.
- Eye protection.

Materials

- $1^1/_2$" X $^3/_{16}$" thick strips of wood for the logs.
- Cardboard base piece for house about 10" X 10" or 8" X 12".
- Thin plywood for the roof. Or cardboard. Or nothing.
- Leather for roof hinges or door hinges.
- Paints, markers, and cloth scraps for decorations.

Construction

1. This is a straightforward "one piece at a time" project with lots of room for creativity. It's about measuring. Hold a "log" up to where you want it to go on the base piece. Mark where it needs to be cut. Cut it. Go back and glue it in place. Repeat this over and over and end up with a house. Leave holes for doors and windows.
2. Make furniture (see furniture projects, page 86).
3. A roof or door may be hinged with small strips of leather and hot glued in place.
4. Decorate.

SAILBOAT LETTER HOLDER

When I was in the 6th grade, I made this letter holder for my mom. For nearly fifty years she used it to hold her bills *(Figure 138)*. The letter holder doesn't have to be a sailboat. It could be a horse, a flower, or any other design from a child's imagination.

Figure 138.
The sailboat letter holder I built for my mom when I was in the 6th grade.

Tools
- Handsaw.
- Vice.
- Eye protection.
- Coping saw.
- Sandpaper.

Materials
- 2 pieces of ¹/₄" plywood 6" square.
- Four small finish nails.
- Oil or paint to suit.
- 1 X 2 about 4" long.
- A little wood glue. White glue will do.

Construction
1. Draw the front and back piece of the letter holder on the wood and cut it out with a coping saw.
2. Sand.
3. Cut the 1 X 2 connector piece. Nail (and glue) this connector to the bottom of the front of the letter holder. Nail the back of the letter holder to the connector.
4. Sand and oil or paint.

WHALE SCULPTURE

My mom liked whales, so when my son Ben was in middle school shop he built her this small whale sculpture *(Figure 139)* for Christmas. Instead of a whale, use another favorite animal.

Figure 139.
A whale sculpture my son Ben built for his grandma.

Tools

- Coping saw.
- Handsaw.
- Vice.
- Drill with $1/4$" bit.
- Eye protection.

Materials

- 1 X 4 about 6" long for the stand.
- A piece of pine large enough for the whale.
- A little white glue.
- Two $1/4$" dowels about 4" long.

Construction

1. Draw out a whale (or other animal) on the soft pine.
2. Cut the whale out with the coping saw (see coping saw, page 29) and sand.
3. Make the bottom part of the stand from the 1 X 4. Round the corners and sand.
4. Fasten the whale to the bottom part of the stand with dowels. First drill two $1/4$" holes in the bottom of the whale about 4" apart and about $3/8$" deep. Cut two $1/4$" X 4" dowels and temporarily put them into the holes in the whale. Hold the whale (with the dowels sticking out) over the 1 X 4 stand and mark the position where the dowels meet the stand. Drill two holes about $3/8$" deep at the marked spots. Assemble the whale to the dowels and to the bottom of the stand to make sure everything fits and looks OK. If you are satisfied with the way it looks, disassemble, put white glue into the holes, and reassemble. Let the glue dry, do any final sanding, and then oil or paint to suit.

MAGNET PENDULUM

The magnet pendulum in *Figure 140* was given to me by my friend Joe Edwards, who helped found Mindport, an amazing little museum (that's not quite the right word) in Bellingham, Washington.

Adult Preparation

A parent, teacher, or volunteer will need to cut a 6" X 6" piece of sheet metal for each project. I have kids carefully sand the edges. Sheet metal is usually available at hardware stores. **Safety Note:** Because it is easy to cut yourself when cutting sheet metal, I cut this stuff into squares. Be careful. Leather gloves are a good idea.

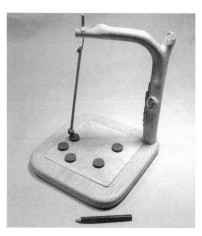

Figure 140.
Joe Edwards gave me this nifty magnet pendulum.

Figure 141.
Appropriate branches are hard to find, so I designed this alternate construction for the magnet pendulum.

Tools
• Tin snips.

• Leather gloves.

Materials
• Galvanized sheet metal.

Kids: Building the Magnet Pendulum

Tools
• Saw.
• A ⁵/₁₆" bit and a ¹/₈" bit.
• Low-temp hot glue gun and glue sticks.

• Vice.
• Clamp.

• Drill.
• Eye protection.

Materials
• ³/₄" pine 8" X 8" base piece.
• A branch about 1" in diameter with an arm sticking out at about 90 degrees *(Figure 140)*

• 6" X 6" piece of galvinized sheet metal.

would be nice. Unfortunately, the perfect branch may be hard to find. If you live near a river, lake, or saltwater, driftwood is a possibility. *Figure 141* shows an alternate construction that works just as well but doesn't look quite so nifty. For this construction, you'll need about 16" of 1" X 1" (which actually measures $3/4$ X $3/4$) and 10" of $5/16$" dowel.

- $5/16$" dowel (for the pendulum, about 8" long).
- Eight $1/2$" (about) magnets available from suppliers on the internet.
- One $1 3/8$" sheetrock screw for the arty version. Or, for the alternate construction, four $1 1/8$" screws.
- An 8-inch piece of nylon string to connect the pendulum to the support.
- A little white glue.
- Four $1/2$" or $5/8$" nails.

Construction

1. Cut out the base piece about 8" X 8".
2. Fasten the sheet metal in the center of the base. Drill four holes in the corners of the metal. Then place the metal in the center of the wood base and pound in the four short nails in the corners.
3. Make the support for the swinging magnet. There are two choices here:
   • If you are using a branch, the arm should stick out over the middle of the base. Cut the thicker part of the branch so the arm is about 7" above the base. Fasten the branch to the base piece with a sheetrock screw (pre-drill the base piece) and a dab of white glue.
   • If you don't have a branch, the pendulum can be supported by a dowel cross piece supported between two uprights. Drill a hole through the top of each upright for the dowel. Fasten the two uprights (1 X 1s, $7 3/4$" long), opposite each other, and in the middle of the base piece. Pilot holes through the bottom of the uprights are a good idea. Place a dab of white glue in the joint before assembling with screws.
4. Drill a hole in the end of the branch (or the middle of the dowel cross piece) from which the pendulum will swing.
5. For the alternate construction, put the dowel cross piece in place between the two uprights. A bit of glue in the holes should keep it in place.
6. Fasten the dowel (the pendulum) to the support. Drill a small hole in the end of the dowel first and tie it to the cross piece with string so it swings freely about $1/2$" above the metal. Too much clearance and the magnets won't attract and repel each other; too little clearance and they'll hit.
7. When the clearance is satisfactory, hot glue one magnet to the end of the dowel. Use lots of glue.
8. To test, spread the rest of the magnets around the metal and swing the pendulum. The pendulum should swing in unpredictable ways as it is attracted to and repelled from the other magnets.

STILTS

One of my favorite childhood projects was stilts *(Figure 142)*. My grandfather built my sister and me a set and set off a frenzy of stilt building. Each new set was higher than the last, until my Grandfather, afraid we'd get hurt, said we couldn't go any higher. Stilt building was even useful as an adult when I built a set for my wife as part of a halloween costume. The following plans show how to make stilts that are adjustable to three different heights. Non-adjustable stilts could be made by replacing the carriage bolts with screws (big strong ones) and glue.

These stilts are designed for 3rd, 4th, and 5th graders. For younger children, make them a bit shorter and lower the steps. For older kids or adults, replace the 1 X 2 with 2 X 2 to carry the extra weight. 2 X 2s will require longer bolts.

While I think stilts are safer than riding a bicycle or playing baseball, there is the possibility of injury. I recommend adult supervision. Help kids choose a safe place to practice. Grass is a good place to start. While it's harder to walk on grass than on cement, it's a lot softer when you fall.

Figure 142.
My son Ben on stilts.

Tools
- Handsaw.
- Eye protection.
- Two crescent wrenches.
- Vice.
- Sandpaper.
- Square.
- Drill and $^1/4$" bit. If you have a $^{17}/64$" bit, use it instead of the $^1/4$" bit. The slightly larger holes will let the bolts slide through the holes easier for marking hole position and adjusting stilt height.

Materials
- About 10 feet of 1 X 2.
- Four $^1/4$" X $4^1/2$" long bolts with matching nuts.
- Eight fender (big) washers to go under the bolt heads and the nuts.
- Latex paint and a small paint brush.
- Eight inches of 2 X 4 for two 4" steps.

Construction *(Figure 143)*
1. Cut the 1 X 2 into two 60" lengths. These are the upright pieces.
2. Cut the 2 X 4 into two 4" pieces to form the step piece that will hold your foot.
3. Drill two holes through each 2 X 4 step. Keep the holes as straight as possible.
4. Draw lines (with the square) across each upright at 6", 12", and 18" for the three different height adjustments.
5. Each step will be held in place by two bolts. Drill the first of two holes in the upright to match one of the holes in the block. To get the holes in the right place, hold the block on top of the 1 X 2 with the top of the block even with one of the lines. Put the bolt through the hole and tap it with a hammer so it leaves a mark on the 1 X 2. Remove the block and drill a hole at the mark. Do the same for the other two positions on the same upright. Repeat the procedure for the second upright with the second block.
6. Drill the second hole in the upright. Fasten the block to the upright with one bolt.

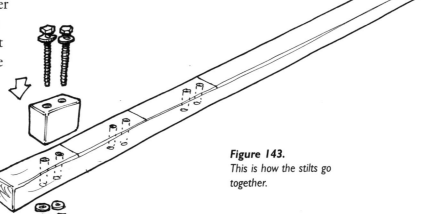

Figure 143.
This is how the stilts go together.

Just as with the first hole, tap the second bolt through the block and leave a mark on the 1 X 2 for drilling. Remove the block and drill the hole. Mark and drill the other two holes and then do the other upright.

7. Fasten each step in place. Tighten the bolts using one wrench to hold the bolt and one to tighten the nut.

Troubleshooting

The hardest part is to keep the holes through the 2 X 4 straight. The holes should start in the middle and end in the middle of the block. If the holes run out too close to one side it's best to try again on another block before drilling the 1 X 2.

Using Stilts

To use the stilts, first make sure the blocks are on tight. At first I tried wing nuts because I thought they would be easier for kids to change. They were easier, but kids couldn't get them tight enough to keep the blocks from moving. That's why I recommend using regular nuts and a wrench to tighten them. *Kids should become competent at the lower adjustment before moving up.* Other than that, it's hard to explain with words how to actually use stilts; a demonstration is the way to go. *Figure 144* shows one way to hold stilts. Reach around the front of the stilts, bending over a bit, with your hands down low, and hold the stilts against your shoulders.

Figure 144.
One way to hold the stilts is to reach around the front of the stilts and pull them against the back of your shoulders.

BIRD FEEDER

Tools

- Handsaw.
- Scissors for cutting string.
- Screwdriver for sheetrock screws.
- Brace with magnetic bit holder and bit for sheetrock screws.
- Hammer.
- Eye protection.
- Drill and 3/16" bit.

Figure 145.
The bird feeder makes a great present for Mom or Dad.

Materials

- 1 X 6 about 10" long for base piece.
- 1 X 4 about 8" long for roof support.
- Wood for the roof. Thin wood is best. Some choices:
    - a. Pieces of leftover wood shingles.
    - b. 1 X 4 X 3/4" resawn (or split) on edge to make two pieces 3/8" thick.
    - c. 1/4" exterior (put together with waterproof glue) plywood.
- Enough 1/4" X 1 1/2" strips for edging around the base.
- Two 1 3/8" sheetrock screws to fasten the base to the roof support.
- Fourteen 3/4" nails to fasten the edging to the base and to fasten the roof to the support.
- Thirty inches of heavy string so the bird feeder can be tied to a branch *(Figure 145).*

Construction

1. Select the base piece and cut to approximately 5¹/2" X 10". Sand.
2. Cut the roof support. This is the boat-shaped piece. First, lay out the shape to be cut. This can be done either by having a pattern for kids to trace (the easy way) or by demonstrating how to lay out the peak so it is equal on both sides, as follows:
   • Draw a line across the board. It should be square to the edge of the board and back about 2¹/2" from one end.
   • Find and mark the center of the board at the end closest to the line.
   • Then connect the center mark to the point(s) where the square line meets the edge of the board *(Figure 146)*. Refer to *Figure 16* (page 27) for how to cut the peak; it is the same as for the bow of a boat.

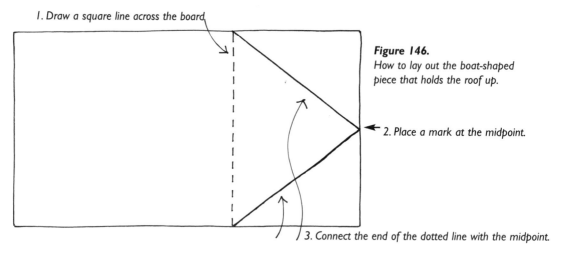

1. Draw a square line across the board

Figure 146.
How to lay out the boat-shaped piece that holds the roof up.

2. Place a mark at the midpoint.

3. Connect the end of the dotted line with the midpoint.

3. Drill a ³/16" hole in the top of the roof support, close to the peak, for the string.
4. Fasten the roof support to the base. Hold the roof support in place and draw around it. In this rectangle, mark the position for two pilot holes. Drill the holes through the base at the marked points. Start the screws (up from the bottom) in the pilot holes so they just barely stick out. Put the roof support piece in the vice, with the peak down between the vice jaws. Hold the base in position over it, and drive the screws into the roof support.
5. Fasten the edging to the base. This is best done one piece at a time. That is, measure one piece and nail it in place. Measure piece number two and nail it in place. Same with the third and fourth pieces.
6. Cut the roof pieces and drill holes in each for the string.
7. Fasten the roof boards to the roof support. This is tricky because it's hard to hold the roof support (it's at an angle) in place as the nails are being hammered in. Drilling pilot holes (same as for the base piece) will make it easier. A helper to hold the bird feeder solidly in place will help, too.
8. Attach the string. It goes down through one roof hole, through the hole in the roof support, and then back up through the other roof hole.

CLIMBING BEAR

The climbing bear is a bear-shaped cutout suspended from two strings which run through angled holes in the bear paws *(Figure 147)*. Children make the bear climb the strings by alternately pulling down on one string and then another.

Tools
- Coping saw.
- Vice.
- Handsaw.
- Sandpaper.
- A drill and $3/16$" bit.
- Eye protection.
- Soldering iron or candle to cut nylon line.

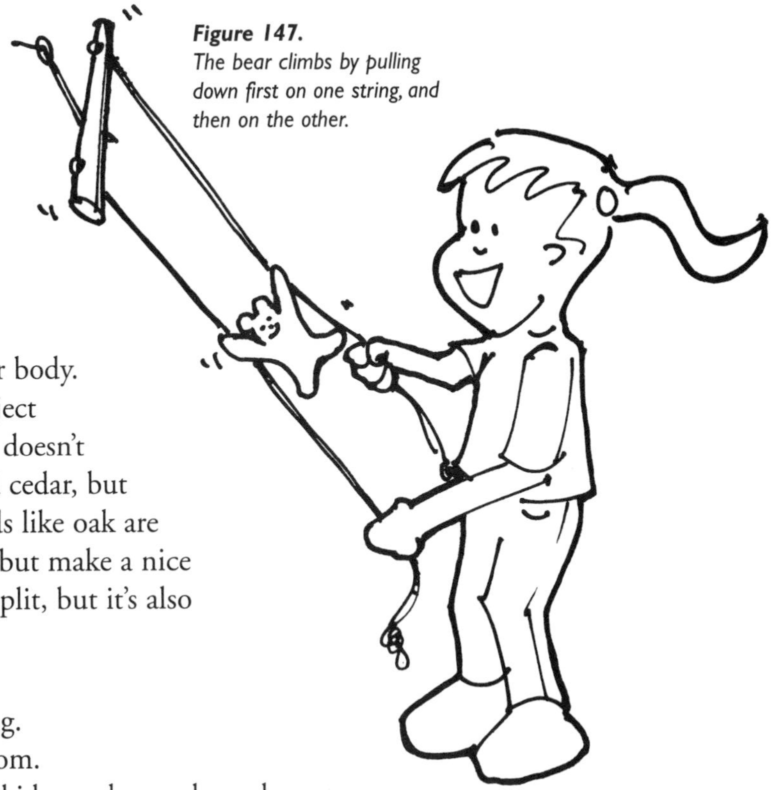

Figure 147.
The bear climbs by pulling down first on one string, and then on the other.

Materials
- 6" X 6" piece of pine for the bear body. Pine is a good wood for this project because it's soft, easy to cut, and doesn't split too readily. I've used fir and cedar, but they split more easily. Hardwoods like oak are harder and more difficult to cut but make a nice climbing bear. Plywood doesn't split, but it's also harder to cut.
- 6" piece of $3/8$" dowel.
- About 13 feet of $1/8$" nylon string.
- Screw or nail to hang the bear from.
- A model of the climbing bear so kids can have a bear shape to trace and see how the string is run. He is about 5" tall and $3^{1}/2$" across.

Construction
1. Trace the bear from the pattern onto the wood *(Figure 148)*.
2. Cut the bear out with a coping saw. Read the section on using the coping saw if you haven't already, page 29. A coping saw is one of the hardest tools for children to use. Kids will need reminders to keep their saw position square and to rotate the bear in the vice as their cut progresses. Reduce coping saw cuts to a minimum by roughing out the bear shape with a regular handsaw. Don't think of cutting out the bear as one long cut in the same direction. Think of short cuts going either direction. Often rotating the bear in the vice will make a cut much easier.

3. Put the bear in the vice and sand. A Surform plane may be appropriate in some of the rougher spots, if they can be reached. Sanding tools can be made to reach awkward places by hot gluing small strips of sandpaper to small sticks and dowels.

4. Drill holes in bear paws. These holes must be put in at the correct angle or the bear won't climb. Draw the hole positions *(Figure 148)* at the correct angle from the pattern. One way to visualize these holes is to place the model bear on the table and slide thin nails through the holes so they stick out on both sides of the hole. Then place the bear on top of the model and draw lines running the same direction as the nails. Position the bear in the vice so the hole angle will be in a comfortable position to drill.

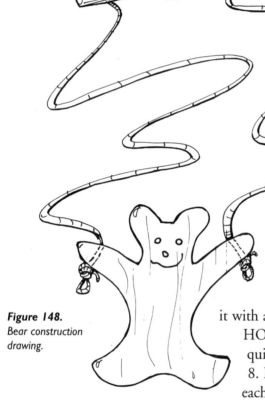

5. Cut the dowel for the rocker arm and mark the position of the holes from the model. One hole goes near each end, and one in the middle.

6. Drill three holes in the dowel. Since it is difficult to start a hole on a round object (the bit wants to slide off), here is a helpful trick: file a cross (an X) with the corner of a file at each hole position and start the hole in the center of the cross.

7. Measure and cut string. The two longer strings should be about 6 feet long and the shorter one about a foot long. Better too long than too short. Nylon line unravels when it is cut with scissors, so melt it with a candle or cut it with a soldering iron. Melted nylon is HOT and will burn if you touch it. Fortunately, it cools quickly. Wait 15 seconds or so before touching it.

Figure 148.
Bear construction drawing.

8. Final assembly. Tie an overhand loop knot in the end of each of the three strings. Run the short string through the center hole on the dowel and tie a figure eight knot so the end can't slip back through. *Figure 149* shows the knots. The bear will hang from this string. Run the longer strings up through the bottom of the bear paws (the overhand loops are below the paws) and then through the bottom of the holes on the dowel. Adjust the long strings so they are equal in length and tie figure eight knots on the top of the dowel.

9. Test and decorate. Hang the bear up from the middle loop and make sure he works. The strings have to be pulled alternately, right then left then right again. Why does the bear climb? The strings run at an angle through holes in the bear's paws. As one string is

pulled, it straightens the hole which lifts the opposite bear arm. Then the second string is pulled and the process repeats. Each time a string is pulled, one arm of the bear climbs a little higher. Releasing tension on the strings will bring Mr. Bear back down.

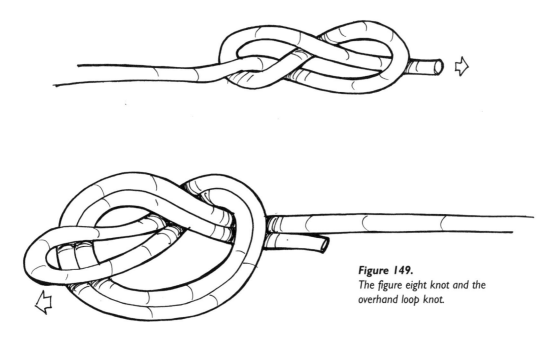

Figure 149.
The figure eight knot and the overhand loop knot.

Troubleshooting

1. The wood splits as it's being cut. This usually happens because the saw is being pushed down too hard or twisted. A light touch is best. Use pine and keep the cut close to the vice.
2. The bear won't climb. Usually this is because the holes were drilled at the wrong angle. Most often there will be enough room to re-drill the holes at the proper angle. If there isn't, glue (with white glue) dowels in the holes, wait till the glue dries, and then re-drill the holes at the correct angle.

ROPE MACHINE

I first saw a picture of the rope machine *(Figure 150)* in a book of projects for kids. At the time I passed it over and handed the book on to my wife, who also worked with children. She purchased a rope machine at a weaving store and found that kids loved it. They were intrigued with choosing the yarn colors and then watching them blend as the rope twisted itself together. With two kids working on it, the finished rope could be cut in half, giving each child a piece to take home. After my wife's success, I began using the rope machine in my shop class. It was so popular, we wore it out and I decided to make one from the directions in the book.

The instructions were marginal and the machine never worked smoothly, so I set out to "do it right," purchasing hardwood, bronze bearings, shafts, and hooks. This time the resulting machine not only didn't work, but was so heavy only a bionic child could lift it. About this time, my brother dropped by and reminisced, "Dad made a rope machine for me when I was a kid. He used coat hangers."

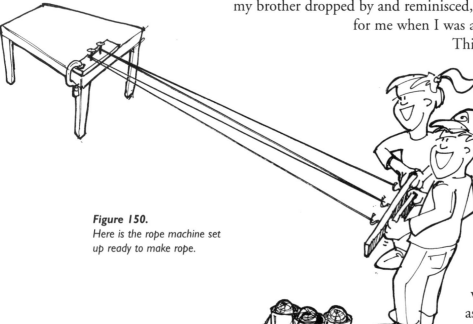

This made sense. While coat hangers are strong, they are also flexible in just the right place. The following instructions detail how to build this rope machine patterned after the 1950s model built by my father for his son, in the spirit of the times, from materials around the house.

Figure 150.
Here is the rope machine set up ready to make rope.

This rope machine works on the same principle as rope walks of tall ship days. It's a good activity to go along with boat building at boat shows, as well as for home, scouts, schools, and children's museums. Everyone will be amazed as the rope winds itself together. Third graders can learn to make rope by themselves. Younger kids will need more supervision. The hardest part of making rope is keeping the yarn from getting tangled or untangling it after it's tangled.

Tools

- Drill.
- Handsaw.
- Tape measure.
- Surform plane.
- Hammer.
- Square.
- Wire cutters or keyhole saw with a hacksaw blade.

- $1/8$" drill bit.
- Vice grips.
- Clamp.
- Sandpaper.
- Two pair of pliers.
- Eye protection.

Materials

- One stiff wire coat hanger. $1/8$" wire, available at hardware stores, will work too.
- Wood: 1 X 2, 26" long. I've used fir, cedar, and maple.
- Wood: $5/4$" (which measures 1") X 2", 10" long. This is for the crank, which turns. If it's thick, it is easier to hold. I usually cut 1" strips on a table saw, but kids could cut 1" sections lengthwise from a 2 X 4 and clean them up with a Surform plane and sandpaper.
- 3 tenpenny nails with large heads.
- Plywood: 6" X 12", $1/2$" or thicker, for the bending jig.

Construction

The rope machine is made up of a handle (the long piece), a crank (the short piece) and three wire hooks. The crank turns the three wire hooks. Each hook twists a separate bundle of yarns. After the bundles are tightly twisted, they're drawn through two nails (the anchor) and allowed to unwind. As they unwind, the separate bundles twist together and make one strand of rope.

1. Make the handle 26" long. Cut 1 X 2 wood to length. Round edges and corners with Surform and sand.
2. Make the crank. Cut the $5/4$" material about 10" long.
3. Lay out the location of the three holes in the handle. The holes should start about 5" from the end, and be 4" apart *(Figure 151)*.

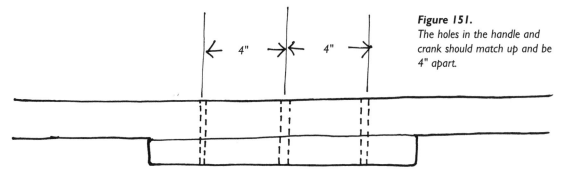

Figure 151.
The holes in the handle and crank should match up and be 4" apart.

4. Drill the holes using the $1/8$" bit. Make sure the holes are drilled as straight as possible. That is, try to hold the drill 90 degrees to the wood while drilling.

5. The holes in the crank are next. They must exactly match the holes in the handle. Place the crank on the handle. Center it over the holes, and clamp it in place. Mark the hole positions in the crank by poking a nail through the already drilled holes (in the handle) and tapping it a couple times. Separate the crank and handle and drill the holes.

6. Cut three 8" wires for the hook/turning mechanisms. Smooth the jagged ends with a file.

7. Make a jig to insure the three wires come out with the same dimensions. The jig is just three nails set in three corners of a 2" square.

8. Bend the wire. I usually do the first wire, and let kids do the others. Lay the 8" wire in the jig as shown in *Figure 152*. The top end of the wire should start near the top edge of the board. Then make the first and second bends sharply around the nails. Remove the wire from the jig, and gently correct the bends to a 90 degree angle.

9. Assemble the crank, the handle, and the wires *(Figure 153)*. Install the long end of one wire into each hole on the handle. Slide the crank over the shorter end of the wires. Before bending the hooks and stops, (the next step) hold the handle and turn the crank. It should rotate smoothly. The flexibility of the wire should compensate for the holes being a bit

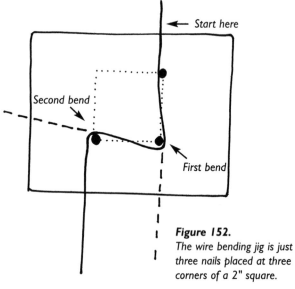

Figure 152.
The wire bending jig is just three nails placed at three corners of a 2" square.

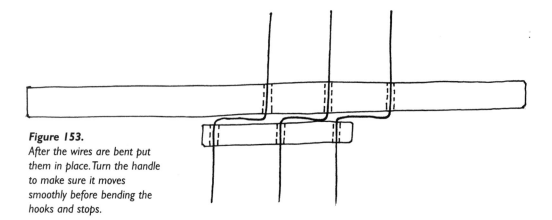

Figure 153.
After the wires are bent put them in place. Turn the handle to make sure it moves smoothly before bending the hooks and stops.

off or the wires not being quite the same. If the handle doesn't rotate freely, go back and figure out why. Is one of the holes at a weird angle? Is one of the wires noticeably different from the others? Are the distances between the holes different? Once the crank will turn freely, go on to the next step.

10. Bend the wires so there will be hooks sticking out of the handle and stops on the back of the crank to keep it from falling off *(Figure 154)*. The stop on the back of the crank has two 90 degree bends. The hook on the handle side is a 45 degree bend and then a series of short bends to make something resembling a hook. I use two pair of pliers. Again, I'll demonstrate how to do the first wire and let the student do the other two.

11. Use two nails of the bending jig for the "anchor". The purpose of the anchor is to hold the other end of the yarn as it is being twisted by the rope machine.

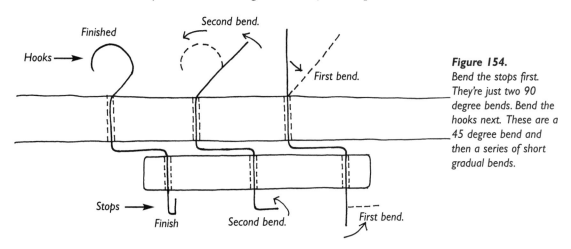

Figure 154.
Bend the stops first. They're just two 90 degree bends. Bend the hooks next. These are a 45 degree bend and then a series of short gradual bends.

Using the Rope Machine

Making rope takes two people. One cranks the rope machine and the other pulls the rope out after the yarn is twisted. When making rope for the first time, an adult will probably need to string the machine and demonstrate how to pull the completed rope through the anchor.

Tools

- Rope machine.
- "Anchor" and clamp. The "anchor" is just two nails.
- Scissors.
- 3 three-lb coffee cans, one for each skein of yarn. Oatmeal cartons or three small paper bags stapled together will work, too.

Materials

- 3 balls or skeins of medium weight yarn. The more color choices you have the more interesting and varied the rope will be. Children love variegated yarn and bright colors.

Set Up

1. Clamp the anchor to a tabletop. Have the kids choose three different colored yarns. Put each skein of yarn in a different container (so they won't get tangled up) on the floor under the rope machine. Tie the three yarns together with an overhand knot.
2. Position two kids about 6 to 10 feet from the anchor. Both children can help hold the rope machine while you are stringing it up. The hooks should face the anchor.
3. Pick up the yarns (they're tied together) and tie them to the closest hook.
4. Starting from hook #1, run the yarn as indicated in *Figure 155.* Have the kids keep a bit of tension on the rope machine and hold it parallel to the anchor.
5. After you have passed the yarn around hook #3, run it back around both anchor nails (as if they were one) and back to your starting point, hook #1, cut it and tie it to the hook. You are ready to make rope!

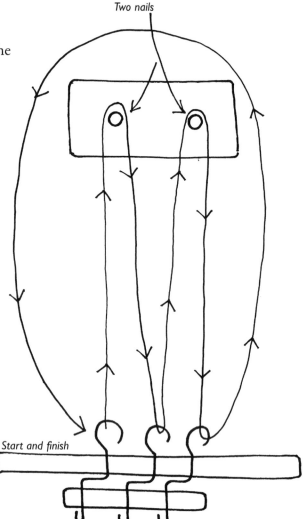

Two nails

Start and finish

Figure 155.
To string up the rope machine, start and end with the same outside hook.

Cranking

1. Start cranking clockwise and continue in the same direction.
2. Keep an even tension on the yarn. As the yarn twists tighter, the operator has to move slowly toward the anchor while still keeping tension on the yarn. Once the three strands have a tight twist and before the twisted strands begin to kink, stop cranking and go on to the next step.

Drawing out the Rope

1. Insert your fingers behind the nails *(Figure156)* and pull the rope toward you.

2. After you have pulled the rope out about a foot, pinch it off with your other hand just behind the nails.

3. Let go with the first hand (left hand in the drawing), and as the three strands unwind, they will twist themselves together into one piece of rope. This is the part everyone likes best. Smooth any kinks out of the newly made rope as you go along.

4. As you pull the rope out, your helper holding onto the crank must walk slowly forward, maintaining an even tension on the yarn. Kids catch on quickly with practice.

5. After all the rope has been drawn out, slip the yarn off the hooks. Tie the ends together with an overhand knot to prevent them from unraveling.

6. Cut the rope into two pieces, one for each rope maker, and again tie off the ends with an overhand knot or the rope will unravel.

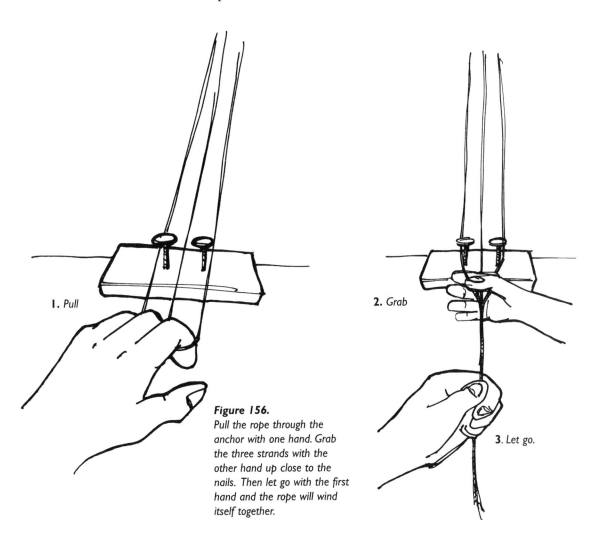

1. *Pull*

2. *Grab*

3. *Let go.*

Figure 156.
Pull the rope through the anchor with one hand. Grab the three strands with the other hand up close to the nails. Then let go with the first hand and the rope will wind itself together.

"NUF" MODEL

The "Nuf" *(Figure 157)* is a real boat designed for kids by Carl Chamberlain. Full sized, it is built from one sheet of 4 X 10 plywood and a few ten foot long 1 X 4s. I once helped 24 kids build 6 "Nufs" in five days. Many of the problems involved in building a real boat are encountered in building the model, so we had the kids build models first. Even if kids don't have the chance to build a real "Nuf", they like the idea of building a model shaped and formed like a real boat. If you are interested in the real "Nuf," the address for plans is on page 198.

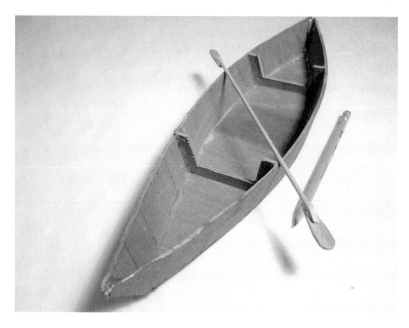

Figure 157.
A model of a "Nuf."

Adult Preparation

A parent, teacher, or volunteer needs to:
1. Make patterns for the side planking and mark the position of the frames *(Figure 158)*.
2. Make a pattern for the frames to the dimensions given *(Figure 159)*.
3. Cut planking into $1^{1}/2$" strips.

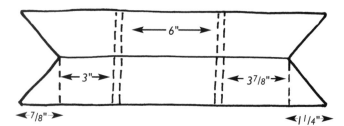

Figure 158.
Side plank dimensions. Each plank is $1^{1}/2$" wide.

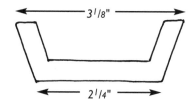

Figure 159.
The dimensions for the frame pattern. The frame is $1^{1}/2$" tall.

Kids: Building the "Nuf" Model

Tools

- Sandpaper.
- Surform plane.
- Drill with small nail ($1/16$") for bit.
- Low-temperature hot glue gun and glue sticks.
- Handsaw and keyhole saw (with hacksaw blade).
- Pliers.
- Vice.
- Eye protection.

Materials

- A piece of $1/8$" plywood, 16" long and 10" wide for each boat. Rotary-cut mahogany (called a door skin) bends easiest but other thin plywood will work. Most lumber yards will have this material.
- Thin wire, about 12" for each boat.
- Shellac (it is nontoxic and dries quickly) to seal the wood. Other sealers will work.
- Latex paint.
- $1/8$" dowel plus small plywood scraps for the paddle ends.

Construction

1. Cut out two side planks. Mark the frame positions on the inside of the planks.
2. Cut out two frames from the pattern.
3. Stack one of the planks on top of the other. Drill two holes at the bow and two holes at the stern. These will be for wiring the two planks together.
4. Wire the ends of the planks together. Cut four pieces of wire about 3" long. Run the wire through the holes (at the ends of the planks) and twist the two ends together.
5. Spread the planks and work the frames into position *(Figure 160)*. This step is a bit tricky, so proceed nice and easy. The frames should be flush (even) with the bottom of the planking. When frames are in position, glue them in place.
6. Glue the ends of the planks together with hot glue. Let the glue dry before going on to the next step.

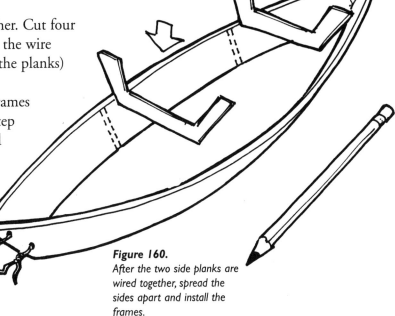

Figure 160.
After the two side planks are wired together, spread the sides apart and install the frames.

7. Flip the boat over and make sure the bottoms of the frames are even with the bottom of the side planking. Use sandpaper or a Surform plane to even them up, if necessary.

8. Cut out the bottom planking. Hold the boat on top of the bottom piece and trace around it. Cut out this piece and glue it on. Add extra glue on the inside to make the bottom stronger. Smooth up the outside joint between the bottom and the sides (the chine) with a Surform plane or sandpaper.

9. Make the paddle about 10" long. Use the $^1/8$" dowel for the shaft and thin plywood scraps for the blades.

10. Seal with two coats of shellac and paint with latex paint. Don't leave the "Nuf" in the water for long periods of time or moisture will get into the wood and the hot glue will come apart.

APPENDIX
TOOL LIST

Here is a list of tools for woodworking with kids. I chose medium quality tools, which work well with kids, but I avoided cheap tools which often bend or break. I haven't included individual prices because they are subject to change, but by comparing prices I was able to purchase everything on this list locally (in 2005) for about $250. That includes a free workbench, which I made from found materials, and an excellent $2 garage sale saw I paid $8 to sharpen.

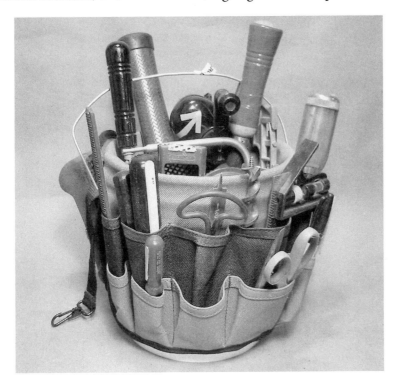

Figure 161.
A tool bag is handy because it organizes tools where you can see them and keeps tools from banging up against one another. A homemade tool box works fine too.

Tool List
- Tool bag *(Figure 161)*. A tool bag is nice because it organizes the tools and keeps tools from banging up against one another, but a homemade tool box works just fine, too.
- Workbench.
- Woodworking vice.
- Handsaw.
- Set of twist drill bits.
- Keyhole saw.
- 13 ounce hammer with curved down claw.
- Small square.
- Tape measure.
- Long nose pliers.
- Crescent wrench.
- Wire cutters.

- Nails and a tray to hold them.
- Center finder.
- Center punch and nail set.
- Kid-sized leather gloves.
- Sandpaper.
- Low-temp hot glue gun plus glue sticks.
- Hold-down clamp for the miter block.
- Brace plus $1/2$" and $3/4$" spade bits for it.
- Screws and a tray to hold them. I use sheet rock screws $7/8$", $1^3/8$". $1^5/8$" and occasionally 2".
- A four-way screw driver (each four-way screwdriver has four different bits).
- Eggbeater-type drill. The Fiskars drill is an option.
- One three-inch clamp (two or three would be nice).

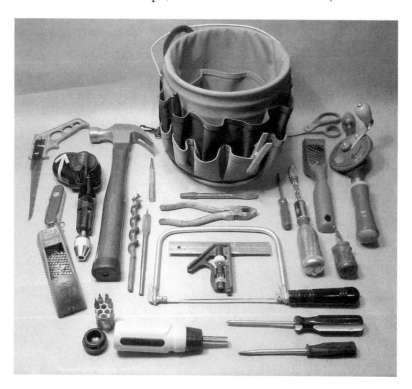

Figure 162.
A tool bag will hold a surprising number of tools.

- Two different-shaped Surform planes: 6" flat and $2^1/2$" curved.
- Magnetic bit holder plus assorted bits to fit.
- Two coping saws to make one two-handled saw.
- 1" roofing nails (big heads).
- $3/4$", 1", $1^1/4$", $1^1/2$" common (normal sized head) nails.
- $1^1/4$" finish (small head) nails for signs.

Duplicates

If you are working with more than two or three kids, you'll need duplicate tools. Ideally, it would be nice for each child to have her own workbench and tools but I've been able to make it work with the following:

- Vices: one for every two kids.
- Different-sized spade bits.
- Countersink with its own handle.
- Saws: one for every two kids.
- Extra blades for the Surform planes.
- Extra saw blades for the keyhole saw and the coping saw.
- More clamps are always useful. For ten kids I have five different clamps.
- Another drill or two, so you don't have to change bits so often and so more than one child can drill at one time.

Nice Additions

- Hand-operated drill press.
- Spiral screwdriver plus bits (2 Phillips, 2 slotted, 3 or 4 different sized drill bits).

Sources for Tools

- A good hardware store often will have almost everything, so you won't need to go to several places, and prices are often better than at the big stores. I bought most of the tools on my list at a very good local hardware store.
- Big home improvement stores. For this tool set, I bought the vice, hammer, drill bit set, and a clamp at one of the big home improvement stores. Interestingly, this store did not carry hand drills or a brace.
- A hardware store which sells used tools. Most larger cities will have one.
- Woodworking catalogs such as Woodcrafters and Woodworker's Supply sell many tools.
- The internet, but you need to know exactly what you are looking for and get some assurance of quality.
- Garage sales are a good source of tools if you know what to look for.

TOOLS YOU CAN MAKE
A Homemade Child-Sized Workbench

A workbench should be sturdy, the proper height, and heavy enough so it won't move around. The bench dimensions should be at least two feet by four feet (bigger is better) and stand 24" high for preschoolers, 27" high for older kids. Two younger children can share one bench but older kids might need a whole bench to themselves *(Figure 163)*.

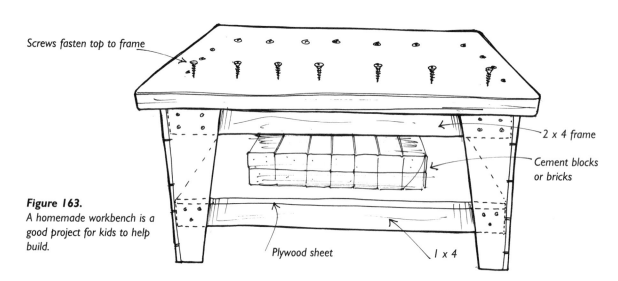

Screws fasten top to frame

2 x 4 frame

Cement blocks or bricks

Figure 163.
A homemade workbench is a good project for kids to help build.

Plywood sheet   1 x 4

The easiest way to make the bench so it won't move around is to weigh it down with cement blocks. You could also screw it to the wall or floor but before doing so, consult a builder.

Tools

- Drill bits.
- Phillips screwdriver.
- Eye protection.
- A brace (and bit) or battery-powered drill.
- A hand drill, or electric (battery or plug in) drill.
- Handsaw. If you know how to use a circular saw, it will make things faster, but there are only a few minutes of actual sawing if your saw is sharp.

- Square.
- Vice.
- Tape measure.

Materials

1. Two 48" 2 X 12s for the top. You could also use 2 X 10s or three 2 X 8s. An old solid-core door also works if cut down to the proper size.
2. 2 X 4s: Two pieces 40" long and two pieces 15" long for the frame under the tabletop. This frame will hold the top pieces together and be the point of attachment for the legs.
3. Twenty-two $2^1/2$" sheetrock screws to fasten the tabletop to the frame and to fasten the 2 X 4 frame together.
4. $^1/2$" plywood: 32" X $22^1/2$" for preschoolers or 32" X $25^1/2$" for late elementary kids. These will be the table legs.
5. Thirty-two $1^1/8$" sheetrock screws to fasten legs together and to the frame.
6. Two 1 X 4s about 40" long. These will run between two legs (the long way) and support a plywood shelf to hold concrete blocks.
7. Eighteen $1^1/8$" sheetrock screws for fastening the 1 X 4 to the workbench legs and for fastening the plywood shelf to 1 X 4 supports.
8. $^3/4$" plywood about 16" X 36" (check actual measurements from your bench) for the shelf which goes on top of the 1 X 4s and holds the concrete blocks.
9. 100-150 pounds of concrete blocks. I prefer the solid ones, $1^1/2$" X $7^1/2$" X $15^1/2$" long. They weigh about 15 pounds and take up less space than the blocks with holes.
10. $^1/8$" (any thickness will work) plywood $17^1/2$" X 36" (check actual measurements from your workbench) to cover the top of the blocks so they may be used as a storage area without damaging tools.
11. Two 8" sections of 1 X 2 for cleats to keep the thin plywood from sliding off the blocks.

Construction

1. Cut the two 2 X 12s (or two 2 X 10s or three 2 X 8s) 48" long *(Figure 163)*.
2. Cut the 2 X 4 into two 40" pieces and two 15" pieces and screw them together at the corners to form a rectangle. The end pieces (the 15" ones) should lap over the longer pieces, giving a rectangle 15" across.
3. Fasten the top pieces to the rectangle with the $2^1/2$" screws. To set this up, put the two top pieces together side by side, lined up evenly at the ends, and center the 2 X 4 rectangle on top of them. Draw around the rectangle on both sides of the 2 X 4s. Take the rectangle off the top pieces and drill 14 holes, equally spaced and halfway between the two lines. Fastening through these holes into the 2 X 4 rectangle will fasten the top to the rectangle.

4. Make the legs from the ¹/2" plywood *(Figure 164)*. First cut plywood into four 8" X 22¹/2" (or 8" X 25¹/2") pieces. Each of these pieces will form one leg after it has been cut into two equal and tapering pieces 5" at the top and 3" at the bottom. Fasten the two tapered pieces together at the corners (5" end up) with the 1¹/8" sheetrock screws. Make all four legs.

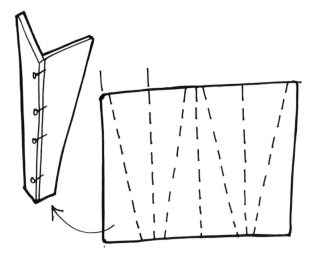

Figure 164.
Strong workbench legs can be built from ¹/2" plywood. The top of the leg is 5" and the bottom is 3".

5. Turn the workbench top upside down and fasten a leg at each corner to the brace/framework with at least four screws per leg.
6. Make the shelf to support the concrete blocks. Fasten one of the 1 X 4s between the front table legs about 6" above the floor. Fasten the other 1 X 4 between the back table legs at the same level as the front 1 X 4.
7. Place the ³/4" plywood on the 1 X 4 supports and fasten with screws.
8. Stack the blocks on the shelf.
9. Cover the blocks with the thin plywood. To keep this plywood in place, fasten two 1 X 2s along the 36" edge of the plywood. These should fit down over the blocks and will keep the plywood from sliding around. The cleats must be at least 15³/4" apart so they will fit over the blocks *(Figure 165)*.

Thin plywood

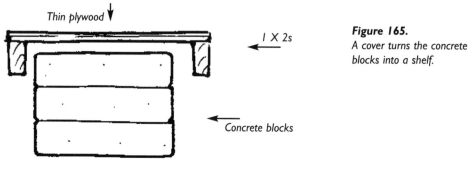

1 X 2s

Concrete blocks

Figure 165.
A cover turns the concrete blocks into a shelf.

THE SCREWDRIVER PRACTICE BOARD

Many children don't know there are different kinds and sizes of screwdriver bits. A child's tendency to reach for the closest screwdriver often results in frustration. I realized I needed to go back a step and give the youngsters practice choosing the proper screwdriver bit and turning it the correct direction *(Figure 166)*.

I went to the hardware store and bought a screwdriver with an array of different bits (slotted, Phillips, square etc.) stored in the handle. I then purchased machine screws (the ones a matching nut threads onto) with different heads to match the bits. Finally, I made a board with holes threaded for the machine screws. Kids choose a machine screw, match it with the proper bit, put the bit in the screwdriver, and turn the machine screw into a hole on the board. They can do this over and over until they have used all the different machine screws and bits.

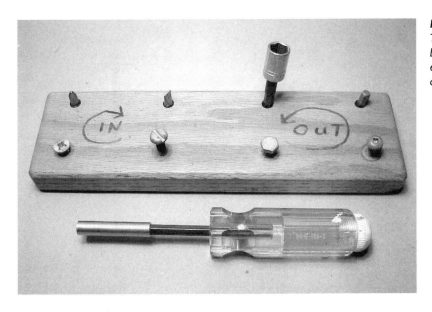

Figure 166.
The screwdriver practice board is a good way to expose very young children to tools.

Tools

- Hammer.
- Drill and 3/8" drill bit.
- Eye protection.
- Screwdrivers to match the machine screws.
- Handsaw.
- Vice.

You can buy several individual screwdrivers to match each machine screw or you can choose one of the newer screwdrivers with interchangeable bits. The bits are cleverly stored in the screwdriver handle. Hardware stores will usually have several to choose from. Find one with bits that remove easily from the handle and install easily in the holder. Avoid screwdrivers with ratcheting mechanisms. They can be unnecessarily confusing. Don't buy cheap screwdrivers! Cheap screwdrivers are made from soft metal and wear out quickly.

Safety Note: bits should slide easily out of the bit holder. Some are quite sticky and children have a tendency to look directly at a bit while they are removing it. If the bit pops out suddenly, it could poke them in the face or eye. Teach kids to point the bit away from their body when changing bits. Another reason for eye protection.

Materials

- Wood, a 1 X 4 about 12" long. Oak or maple is nice.
- Four $1/4$" tee-nuts, *(Figure 167)*. A tee-nut is an odd shaped nut which fastens to wood with prongs. From the top it looks like a round (not hex) nut with portions of the circle bent up to form the prongs.
- $1/4$" machine screws with different type heads to match the screwdriver bits in the handle of the screwdriver.

Figure 167.
The machine bolts thread
into this tee-nut.

Construction

1. Drill four equally spaced $3/8$" holes completely through the 1 X 4.
2. Tap a tee-nut, so the points will bite into the wood, into each hole.
3. Draw two $3/4$" circles on the top of the board, one with an arrow pointing clockwise (labeled "in") and the other with an arrow pointing counterclockwise (labeled "out"). Even if kids can't read, "in" and "out" written inside the circles will help them remember the correct direction to turn the screw. Some screwdrivers have as many as 14 different bits, which is too many for young children to start with. Put some away. I usually start with a small and large Phillips, a small and large slotted, a $1/4$" drive with a small socket and one more unusual bit like a square drive. Kids enjoy this activity. They like the drill bits tucked away in the screwdriver handle. They like matching the drill bits with the screws.

HOMEMADE MITER BLOCK

The miter block will help kids make straight cuts. It's made from two short pieces of 4 X 4. The 4 X 4s are mounted on a piece of plywood and separated by a saw cut. Older kids can make the miter block to use at home *(Figure 168)*.

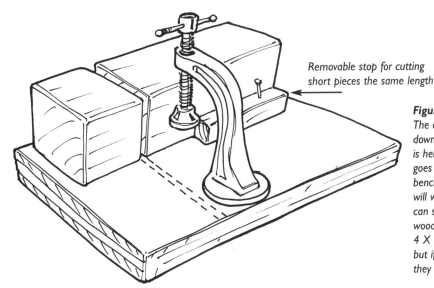

Removable stop for cutting short pieces the same length

Figure 168.
The clamp (called a hold-down clamp) in this picture is held down by a bolt that goes through the work-bench. A regular C-clamp will work, too. Older kids can sometimes hold the wood tight against the 4 X 4 without a clamp, but if the wood moves, they need a clamp.

Tools
- Saw.
- Drill.
- Eye protection.
- Brace with screwdriver bit.
- Screwdriver.
- Vice.
- Square.

Materials
- 3/4" plywood 10" X 6$\frac{1}{2}$".
- 4 X 4 about 10" long.
- Nine 1$\frac{5}{8}$" sheetrock screws.
- Two small finish nails to hold the plywood and 4 X 4 together.
- A hold-down clamp is good for younger kids. It helps them hold the wood so it won't move. Older kids can use a C-clamp, or try to get by without a clamp.

Construction
1. With a square, draw a line completely around the 4 X 4, dividing it into two pieces. This will be the cut that guides the saw.
2. Draw a line square to the edge of the plywood to meet up with the lines around the 4 X 4 *(Figure 168)*.

3. Place the plywood on top of the 4 X 4, matching the lines, and tack it in place with the finish nails. Then drive three screws down through the plywood on each side of the line. Keep all screws and nails away from the line so later the saw will not run into the screws.
4. Fasten the miter block to the workbench with screws. Countersink the screws below the surface of the plywood so they won't damage any wandering saw teeth.
5. Cut completely through the 4 X 4, following the lines previously marked. Since this cut will be the guide for all subsequent cuts, it must be straight.

Using the Miter Block

Here are the steps I demonstrate to each child:
1. Make a pencil mark on the wood where the cut is to be made.
2. Start with the blade of the saw in the cut and the handle resting on the top of the 4 X 4 *(Figure 169)*.

Figure 169.
The saw should rest on top of the miter block before a cut is started, and after a cut is finished.

3. Clamp the wood tight against the 4 X 4 with the pencil mark directly in front of the slot. If the wood is not tight against the 4 X 4 it will move, no matter how tightly clamped. If it moves, it will be hard to cut.
4. Make the cut.
5. **Safety Note:** Put the saw back in the starting position *(Figure 169)* before the wood is removed. If the saw is left dangling with the handle over the edge of the workbench, it can flip out onto the floor and possibly hit someone on the way down.
6. Remove the wood.
7. To cut several pieces the same size, like dowels for table legs or sides for a box, here is a simple trick: mark the first piece and set it in the miter block, as outlined above. Then tack a scrap of wood at the end of the piece being cut. The scrap wood acts as a stop for the next piece so any piece pushed against the stop will end up exactly the same length as the first piece.

A HOMEMADE VICE

A friend showed me a nifty vice his grandfather showed him. You can make it out of scrap materials in a few minutes. It is not as versatile as a mechanical vice, but it works well for many applications. Older kids can build these so they can do woodworking at home. If you need several vices for an event, such as boat building at a children's fair, a woodworker could build ten or fifteen of these quickly and cheaply.

Two pieces of wood, one rectangular, the other wedge-shaped, are fastened with screws to a plywood base which is in turn fastened to a workbench. A loose wedge-shaped piece of wood is then tapped in, to hold the wood by friction, or tapped out, to release it. Different sized wedges allow the vice to hold different sized wood *(Figure 170)*.

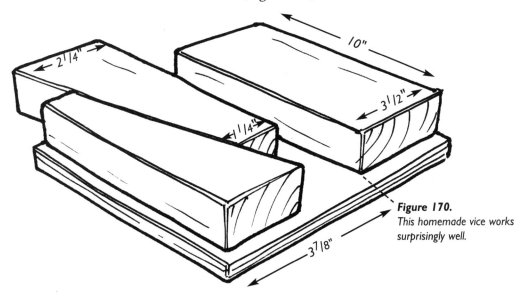

Figure 170.
This homemade vice works surprisingly well.

Tools

- Vice.
- Screwdriver to match screws.
- Clamp.
- Handsaw.
- Hammer.
- Drill and drill bit.
- Brace and bit for driving screws.
- Hand or Surform plane.
- Eye protection.
- A rip saw for cutting the wedges is nice but a crosscut saw will work. Or have someone with a band saw precut these wedge-shaped pieces.

Materials

- Hardwood (oak or maple) would be good, about 20" long and 3¹/₂" wide. A more disposable vice can be made from just about any 2 X 4. Look for one without knots, if possible. Softer wood will work for a while but may eventually split.

- ³/4" plywood about 6" X 10".
- Eight 2" sheetrock screws.
- Two 1¹/4" finish nails.
- Coarse sandpaper, 60 grit.

Construction

1. Cut the hardwood block to the dimensions in *Figure 170.* Plane the angled part of both wedge-shaped pieces flat and sand them with coarse sandpaper to rough up the gripping surface.
2. Mount one of the wedge pieces at the lower right hand corner of the plywood, parallel to the edge of the plywood. Clamp it in place and then fasten it with screws.
3. Screw the rectangular block in place, parallel to, and 3⁷/8" up from the bottom edge of the plywood *(Figure 170).*
4. Test the vice by putting a piece of wood between the rectangular block and the movable wedge *(Figure 171).* Tap the wedge to the right with a hammer until the wood becomes tight. To loosen the wood, tap the wedge back the other way. Since the small end of the wedge is recessed and difficult to hit with a hammer, use a small piece of wood or dowel as an extension to reach it.

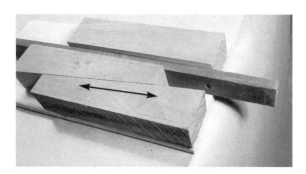

Figure 171.
The darker wood held by this homemade vice is ready to cut.

TAKE-APART

You certainly don't need to take things apart in order to do woodworking, but I've included it because it's a great complimentary activity. I started doing take-apart with kids because it was another way to practice with tools and provided interesting parts for sculpture. Later I realized the problem solving involved in take-apart was not that different from trying to figure out how to put something together out of wood. As a side benefit, take-apart also led to lessons about electricity and recycling *(Figure 172)*.

Figure 172.
Take Apart is a favorite activity of many kids. Here Parker is beginning work on an old tape deck.

Jennifer Fryer

Tools

- Eye protection.
- Wire cutters.
- A brace with a magnetic bit holder and an assortment of bits.
- Pliers.
- Large and small Phillips and slotted screwdrivers.

Materials

Something to take apart. A small tape deck is good for younger kids. VCRs are ideal. A typewriter is good for advanced taker-aparters. I've also used radios (take the tubes out of the old ones), bigger tape decks, movie projectors, record players, and drills. Do not take TVs apart, because they are dangerous.

Safety Note: I limit take apart to two or three kids per object. Children must be closely supervised when taking anything apart. Cut off any electrical cords before starting, and explain about shocks. Remove any glass tubes or bulbs. Consult a technician if there is any question about whether a piece of equipment can be safely disassembled. If kids get frustrated, they want to beat or pry, which is dangerous. Use this opportunity to show them that ingenuity can work where force doesn't.

MECHANICAL PUZZLES

Two parts of learning to build are: 1) seeing that things are made up of pieces and 2) knowing these pieces need to be assembled in some sort of order. You can tell kids this, but they won't hear it. On the other hand, if kids practice the following mechanical puzzles, they absorb the lesson without even knowing it.

The most interesting reaction to these activities (which children accept as puzzles) came from a teacher. I had volunteered to take my puzzle collection, some folk toys, and science equipment to my son's classroom. I spread my collection around and let everyone choose their own project. The teacher, Julie, chose the faucet and asked what she was suppose to do with it. I showed how the gate opens as the handle is turned and told her it was a puzzle. Take it apart and put back together. So she did. She was excited and exclaimed to the kids around her, "Look at this! See how this works." She was engrossed in the mechanics of a faucet. The principal came in. Julie said "Rob, come over here and look at this." I could see Rob had other things on his mind, but she made him come over and listen to her explain how a faucet worked. By merely taking apart and reassembling the faucet, Julie was able to make a small part of the mechanical world less intimidating.

The Little Hammer with Nesting Screwdrivers

I saw a box of these little hammers at the hardware store and it reminded me that my father had given me one like it when I was young. I bought one for my own kids and they proceeded to take it apart and put it back together so many times I took it to my preschool shop class.

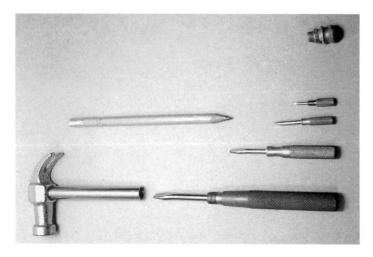

Figure 173.
The little hammer hides four screwdrivers in the handle.

For younger kids I'll take the hammer completely apart, laying the parts in a row, and reassemble it, working backwards, last piece first and first piece last. Laying each piece in order, in a row, is a habit that will keep parts organized when attempting more difficult projects like the faucet and the flashlight. Kids will often take the little hammer apart and put it back together several times. They especially like to show off reassembling it for Mom or Dad *(Figure 173)*.

The Faucet

At the hardware store, I bought an eight-piece brass gate valve, or faucet, about 8" tall. Kids like the feel and size of it. They like to turn the handle and watch the gate inside the faucet open and close.

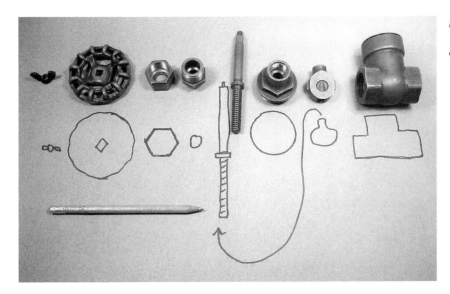

Figure 174.
A faucet is just a three-dimensional puzzle.

To make the faucet easier to put back together and to teach children to keep pieces in order, I drew a pattern of the parts (in the order they came apart) on a piece of cloth. The activity is for children to take the faucet apart, match the pieces to the proper shapes on the canvas and then, working backwards, last piece first and first piece last, put it back together. This is a difficult puzzle the first time. One piece is reverse threaded (turned counterclockwise to tighten) and, not surprisingly, nearly everyone has difficulty with it. The other common difficulty is putting pieces on upside down. If a piece doesn't fit, try turning it over.

After kids can reassemble the faucet using the canvas guide, sometimes I challenge them to put the guide away and try it, still laying the pieces out in order. After they can assemble the faucet without the guide, I'll challenged them to mix the pieces up and try it. If they need help, they can always go back to the canvas pattern. It's amazing to watch a 4- or 5-year-old take the faucet apart, mix all the pieces up, and then put it back together *(Figure 174)*.

The Flashlight

Materials
- A good quality flashlight that comes apart at both ends. It should have a plastic, not a glass, lens.
- Batteries for the flashlight.
- A piece of light-colored cloth (felt or canvas) big enough to hold all the flashlight pieces laid out in a row.
- A small piece of sandpaper (220 grit) to lightly sand the ends of the batteries and/or contacts.

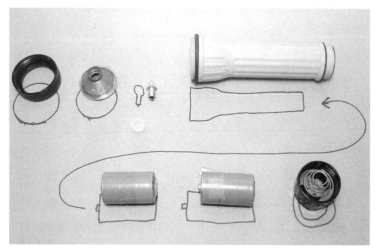

Figure 175.
The flashlight is ready to be put back together.

Figure 176
Summer is taking the flashlight apart.

What to Do

Make a guide to keep the parts in their correct order as the flashlight is disassembled *(Figure 175)*. Take the flashlight apart and set the pieces in order as they come apart, on the cloth. Draw around each piece onto the cloth with a felt tip pen. The activity is for kids to take the flashlight apart, placing each piece on its corresponding shape on the cloth. Then the job is to reassemble the flashlight. The test is, does it work? Common mistakes are putting the batteries in backwards, not having the bulb in properly (be careful of the glass), and not having the threads together straight or tight.

As an added activity you can get a battery checker (electronics supply store) and have children make sure the batteries are OK before assembling the flashlight.

The Dial (or Button) Telephone

In this day and age of cell phones, children are intrigued by the insides of the older dial or button telephones. They especially like the bell which they can ring manually. The cord, the ear and mouth piece, the bell, the hold button apparatus, and the dial or push button mechanism can all be removed and are relatively easy to get back in the right place. Children can also remove and replace wires. It doesn't matter if they don't get them back in the right place. The idea is to see how the major components fit together and not to worry about every last piece. Have a tray to contain the parts and a small box for the screws. If the noise from the bell disturbs others, stuff a small rag under the bell to muffle the sound *(Figure 177)*.

There is usually at least one whiz kid who can help others if they need it. Although small pieces do get lost, I've used the same phone for over three years and the important parts are still there.

Safety Note: Inside phones with buttons, there are tiny glass light bulbs which light up the buttons. Take the phone apart yourself first and remove these, so the kids won't accidentally break them.

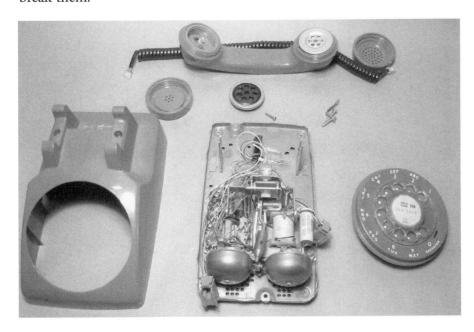

Figure 177.
The dial telephone has lots of interesting pieces to take apart and put back together.

The Door Lock

I found an old door lock at a garage sale and cleaned it up. I replaced one side with a piece of clear plastic so the inner lock mechanism was visible. I painted the inside of the lock white, and each individual piece a different color. Then I set the lock in a mini-door frame. It was hard not to appreciate how the parts fit together and worked. What happens when the door knob is turned? How does this open the door? How does the lock work? Why will one key work and not another?

Kids use the door lock on three levels. First, they just like to open and close and lock and unlock the door, watching how the pieces interact. Then some of the older kids like to take the lock apart and put it back together like a puzzle. And lastly, they like to try to pick the lock with a bent paper clip *(Figures 178 and 179)*.

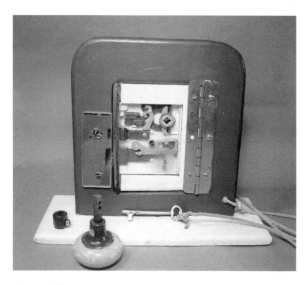

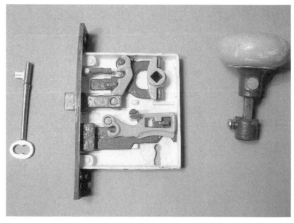

Figure 179.
This door lock is made up of puzzle like pieces.

Figure 178 .
I set the door lock in a small door frame. I removed the door knob to make the working pieces more visible for this picture and for Figure 179.

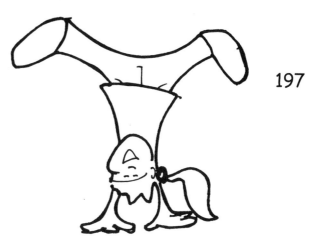

BIBLIOGRAPHY

Bingham, Fred P. *Boat Joinery and Cabinetmaking*. International Marine/Ragged Mountain Press, 1993.

Don't let the title scare you. If you don't know much about woodworking, the first six chapters of this book are a great introduction to tools. The chapters on hand tools begin where my book leaves off. There are also good chapters on hand electric tools and stationary power tools, both of which could be used to do some of the prep work for the projects in this book.

Palmer, Bruce. *Making Children's Furniture and Play Structures*. Workman Publishing Co., 1974.

Although many of the projects in this book are clever and interesting, I've only built the cardboard dome, which alone makes this book worthwhile. Directions are given for constructing a six-foot diameter dome from 10 hex-shaped pieces and 6 pentagon-shaped pieces. The pieces can be fastened with little wing nuts and bolts or glued and stapled. I've helped kids do this several times. Kids love this project. The only qualm I have with the instructions is the author suggests that kids use mat knives to cut out the cardboard. I set them up with small handsaws, which are safer.

Reader's Digest Association. *The Reader's Digest Complete Do-It-Yourself Manual*. 1973.

My edition is 1973, but new editions are published every few years. As the title suggests, this book is not just about woodworking, but I recommend the sections on hand tools, power tools, wood, and fasteners. The rest of the book tells how to build or fix just about every part of your house, which isn't pertinent to working with kids but with it, you could learn how to use the tools necessary to rebuild your house from the ground up.

Starr, Richard. *Woodworking with Kids*. Taunton Press, 1982.

This is a wonderful book about woodworking with kids. Great "big picture" of woodworking with kids (in a public school), wonderful pictures, and lots of ideas. The focus is on middle school shop, so most of the projects are more complicated than this book. The tool section takes up where my book leaves off. A good book for woodworkers to see what another woodworker has done.

Walker, Lester. *Carpentry for Children*. Overlook Press, 1982.

Kids like and are capable of building larger more complicated projects. This book gives examples and directions for how four friends built a workbench, a raft, and a coaster car, to name a few of the larger projects. Great illustrations.

Walker, Lester. *House Building for Children*. Overlook Press, 1988.

Similar to *Carpentry for Children* but the focus is on kid-sized houses.

"Nuf" Plans.

These are plans for the full sized "Nuf". These plans do not include step-by-step instructions, although there is a building sequence list. I've helped both 6th graders and 8th graders build this boat. They were pretty much able to do everything once they were shown how. As part of family boat building (that is, parents and the kids building together), Carl Chamberlain, the designer, has helped third graders (and a parent) successfully complete this boat in a weekend.

Plans are available from:
Basic Boats
Carl Chamberlain
PO Box 709
Port Townsend, WA 98368-0709
360 • 385 • 5772.
email: basicboats@cablespeed.com

Launch day for James Nicholson and the Nuf he built with his grandfather.

Ken Brown

Builder Boards

Jack McKee. Hands On Books, 1997.

This book, written for adults, tells how to build a set of notched boards (like giant notched popsicle sticks) that children use to construct their own play-house. One chapter describes 8th grade students constructing a set of Builder Boards for the local women's care shelter.

Available from:
Jack McKee
1117 Lenora Court
Bellingham, WA 98225

For more information:
<home.earthlink.net/~mchkee>
Phone: 360 • 671 • 9079
Fax: 360 • 714 • 0774
email: mchkee@earthlink.net

David Scherrer

About the Author

JACK McKEE has worked as a mechanic, remodeled houses, built small boats, and designed equipment used by children's museums, schools, and preschools. His articles have appeared in *Home Education, Tech Directions, Early Childhood Today,* and *Wooden Boat.* He teaches woodworking to kids and **"Woodshop for Kids,"** a workshop for teachers. He lives in Bellingham, Washington, with his wife, Candy Meacham. His two sons, Ben and Andrew, who started him working with kids, now work on sailing ships.

David Scherrer

About the Illustrator

RUSTY KEELER lives in the woods of upstate NY and likes to draw pictures. When he's not hiking behind his studio he spends his time helping communities create environmental playscapes which he has built all over North America and in China. Rusty has his own book called *EarthPlay.* Rusty is married to artist Annemarie Zwack. For more information about Rusty Keeler, visit: www.earthplay.net

About the Book Designer

PADDY BRUCE, artist/designer, lives in both the wilds of greater Bellingham and the civilized city of Victoria, BC. Personal ping-pong is one of her favorite pastimes as well as sailing and hiking.

Look for her book *Milagros: A Book of Miracles,* published by HarperSanFrancisco. You can see her illustration work at her website, www.paddybruce.com.

Bill Sodt

INDEX